CLOUD CU{

An Anthology of Favourite Poems

from the parishioners of Shotteswell,

Warmington, Radway and Ratley in

Warwickshire.

Edited by Luise Gunter and Tina Lamb

LIVE WIRE BOOKS

All profits from the sale of this anthology will be donated to the Edgehill Churches of Shotteswell, Warmington, Radway and Ratley.

Further copies of this book may be obtained from Tina Lamb The Rectory, Warmington, Banbury, Oxon. OX127 1BT www.edgehillchurches.co.uk

ISBN No: 0-9542860-9-X

A catalogue record for this book is available from the British Library.

First published in November 2005 by
Live Wire Books,
The Orchard,
School Lane,
Warmington,
Banbury,
Oxon.
OX17 1DE

info@livewirebooks.com
www.livewirebooks.com

Cover illustration by Jennie Boyle

Illustrations by members of the Shotteswell Art Group and other artists in the Benefice.

Printed in Great Britain by Antony Rowe Ltd. Eastbourne

Dedication

Cloud Cuckoo Land is lovingly dedicated to
Luise Gunter by her fellow editor, Tina Lamb.

September 2005

FOREWORD

Back at the end of 2004, whilst putting together the framework of my funeral service, I began to realise how much more effectively the poems I was considering using expressed what I was trying to say about my life than practically any other artistic medium. It set me thinking that others may have long discovered this simple truth and that there could be a treasure trove of ideas and seams of creativity 'out there' which might be tapped for some useful purpose as well as to gratify my own curiosity .

After casually mentioning my thoughts to Tina Lamb, to my surprise, she turned out to be something of a poetry fiend herself. She agreed to join with me in putting together an anthology derived from poems suggested by residents in the Edgehill benefice with the charitable objective of raising money for each of the four benefice churches of which CLOUD CUCKOO LAND is the final result.

Tina may have regretted her early eagerness to be involved as the project became more complicated (as all such undertakings are wont to do). In particular, the thankless chasing of copyright holders to plead for permission to publish their poet's work at no cost in the aid of a good cause fell mostly on her. We had no idea at commencement that the rule for poetry copyright is that it continues until 70 years after death of the poet unless he/she was first published posthumously when the clock starts then. Tina ended up having to do far more than her expected share of the work as my health declined further, although I did manage to squeeze marrying Chris at St Laurence's, Shotteswell somewhere in between!

When we sent out the original letter of request for everyone's favourite poem at Christmas, asking for it to be returned by late January, both of us had serious doubts about whether we would find enough material and if there would be enthusiasm in the villages sufficient to make up a book. Right from the start, it seemed important to have a mixture of favourite poems and own compositions even though this might theoretically lead to variable quality of submission.

Throughout, our aims have centred round the concept of 'taking part' in some form or another rather than being high brow which might lead to us rejecting contributions in the pursuit of excellence. As it's turned out, not only the quantity but also the quality has exceeded anything we could have reasonably hoped to have achieved in such a random exercise.

After some last minute pushing and cajoling, we were thrilled to be able to have a considerable amount of suggestions to sift through from all the villages. Contributors ranged in age from five to ninety plus. And it was at this point that the editorial tough choices had to be made. Some people sent us loads of high quality ideas whilst others forwarded just a single idea. This led us to ensure that at least one original composition per person be included although in some cases we could have put in a complete life's work had space permitted! Where several people have suggested the same poem, all are credited with its choice. The emphasis is to make sure that everyone who has taken the trouble to get involved is included in some way.

The next set of decisions we made was to allocate the best drawings to the chosen poems. Credit should go to Valerie Ingram for involving the Shotteswell village hall Monday evening art group in this project. After Tina and I had decided which poems were suitable for illustrating, they were then distributed amongst the art class members who undertook their own interpretation of the subject matter. Any works needing an illustration which no student had selected were polished off promptly by their tutor **Nick Baldwin.** In addition, some other poems have been ably illuminated by the nominating residents, one or two of whom are professionally competent, benefiting the anthology with a variety of artistic interpretation and stimulating drawings as well as a wide diversity of poetry.

When the BBC undertook a similar exercise 10 years ago, they were overwhelmed by the popularity of a particular war poem which had featured that year 'Do not Stand at my Grave and Weep'. Our equivalent on a much smaller scale was appropriately Betjeman's Diary of a Church Mouse.

I quote the BBC's 'prime, first past the post, poll position' poem below because, although not much cited in our list of suggestions, I think it is still a universal favourite and no anthology would be complete without it. It is strange though, the way thinking about death brings the poetic urge to the surface in so many!

Do not stand at my grave and weep;
I am not there. I do not sleep.
I am a thousands winds that blow.
I am the diamond glints on snow.
I am the sunlight on ripened grain.
I am the gentle autumn rain.
When you awaken in the morning's hush.
I am the swift uplifting rush
Of quiet birds in circled flight.
I am the soft stars that shine at night.
Do not stand at my grave and cry;
I am not there. I did not die.

In fact there has been a tremendous variety in the types and styles of material offered. Although as a former county councillor for three out of the four villages in years past, I thought I knew the villages well and had anticipated that the benefice 'cultural platter' might range from the frankly remote and off-beat to the 'poetry pops' and on to those with an element of - lets politely call it - 'kitsch' but was not prepared for the equivalent to a cultural 'full fat' diet that was the portfolio of suggestions from which we had to choose.

Here, modern poetry is infinitely more popular than the old traditional poems all of us were drilled or force-fed in our school days although, of course, many of these are featured in this anthology. For Tina and me, the main difficulty that emphasis on more recent authors created was that of the copyright with more than 60% of the offerings still eligible where full fees for a number of the poems would have exceeded £400 to £500 each depending upon length.

Inevitably, in the making of our final selection, we will have disappointed some folk. Being an editor sounds glamorous but just means that you take on the responsibility to annoy everyone equally!

Where a poem or poems were written by residents, it is of fine quality and worthy but a number of poems were unattributed, often found in a newspaper or passing in front of you in life's busy twirl, hitting a chord and tarrying a while leaving the author to move on to similarly affect someone else at another time and in another place. Very romantic - but frequently leading us to long and usually fruitless chases. We are obliged in law to carry out all reasonable means to find out who the author is and seek their permission to publish and if unsuccessful put in a statement to that effect. This has been added to our list of permissions and omissions elsewhere in the book.

Selfishly, my personal need in undertaking the project has been fulfilled 'in spades'. It has opened my mind to many new works, some I think I should have known already and many I would never have had a chance to meet, were it not for this anthology. Our book includes works by French, American and Australian poets to name but a few of the nationalities represented. For me it has increased my appetite to read more and experience the power of verse which continues to surprise and works on so many different levels and it is to be hoped that it has this effect on those who pick it up.

For example, in one of the versions of the poem below written by Leo Marks, the spy Violette Szabo was able to tell her SOE controller that she had been captured by the enemy during her last mission to France in 1944 and was transmitting under duress. By dint of change of word so slight – the receiving agents in London could tell – can you?

The life that I have is all that I have
And the life that I have is yours.
The love that I have of the life that I have
Is yours and yours and yours.
A sleep I shall have, a rest I shall have
And death will be but a pause
For the years I shall have in the long green grass
Are yours and yours and yours.

✻

The life that I have is all that I have
The life that I have is yours
The love that I have of the life that I have
Is yours and yours and yours.
A sleep I shall have, a rest I shall have
Yet death will be but a pause
For the peace of my years in the long green grass
Will be yours and yours and yours.

*

The love that I have is all that I have
And the love that I have is yours.
The life that I have is all that I have
And the love that I have of the life that I have
Is yours and yours and yours.
The sleep I shall have, in the death I shall have, is your
For the peace that I have in the long green grass
Will be yours and yours and yours.

It would have not been natural if this exercise had not thrown up which poem was my favourite (apart from the one that I submitted) – a difficult task indeed. My husband, Chris was particularly moved by 'Love' by Thomas a' Kempis (1380 - 1471) – it was a late addition to the anthology. He and I decided to use it in our wedding ceremony and to put it onto our thank you cards. The sentiments are apt and cut close to my heart. The second verse describes a way of loving which, although meant to describe sacred love for God, is so like Chris and the open and brave way in which he loves me especially in these difficult circumstances. He puts me and I think many others to shame.

Love feels no burden, thinks nothing of trouble,
Attempts what is above its strength,
Thinks nothing impossible.
Though weary, love is not tired;
Though alarmed, it is not confounded;
But as a lively flame and burning torch,
It forces its way upwards,
And securely passes through all.

It would be difficult to set out all the people who deserve a thank you for their help and assistance in putting this work together – so I'm not going to try! It's been a labour of love and an experience I would not have missed for all the world. As the poem says 'Love …. thinks nothing impossible'.

So here's to CLOUD CUCKOO LAND, a tribute to the efforts of many, a statement of the choice of hundreds and with a little luck, if we've got it right …a jolly good read!!

Luise Gunter
15th June 2005

Contents

Cloud

Contents

Cuckoo

Contents

Land

CLOUD

Cargoes

Quinquireme of Nineveh from distant Ophir
Rowing home to haven in sunny Palestine,
With a cargo of ivory,
And apes and peacocks,
Sandalwood, cedarwood, and sweet white wine.

Stately Spanish galleon coming from the isthmus,
Dipping through the tropics by the palm-green shores,
With a cargo of diamonds,
Emeralds, amethysts,
Topazes, and cinnamon, and gold moidores.

Dirty British coaster with a salt-caked smoke-stack
Butting through the Channel in the mad March days,
With a cargo of Tyne coal,
Road-rails, pig-lead,
Firewood, iron-ware, and cheap tin trays.

John Masefield
1878 – 1967

To Grandmother

A bright light all around me,
And a deep happiness filling me.
I laugh, I jump, I sing, I shout for joy.
For this is a joyous place, and God is with me.

Calm, still lake of water, all still and like glass.
The sun peeps over the hills, and a brilliant light
Shines over the water to me, laughing for joy.
For this is a joyous place and God is with me.

Waving green grass, on a hill,
I lie in it and think, looking in to the blue sky.
Joy is all around me, and time flies.
For, Grandmother, this is a joyous place, and God is with me.

Time, here is like nothing on earth,
And I am soon with my loved ones.
I am happy, free, and clothes in white.
For this is a joyous place and God is with me.
Happy, Forever and Ever,

Amen.

Sophie Large (1978 – 1998) when age 12

Winter Thoughts

Head bent against the wind
Boots encased in cold, wet mud that clings and weights them down,
I climb the hill.
I pause and look across barren, brown, bleak fields.
The sky is leaden grey and fine mist dampens the air.
Shrivelled, desiccated fruits of autumn cling limp in black hedgerows
And like the fields, my heart too, is empty, tired, half dead.
Sun and summer have become a vague memory and
Laughter, a friend who seldom visits
Once carefree, now careworn.

I look around and whistle to my far off dog.
Looking up, he sees me, wags his tale and bounds excited up the hill,
And I smile and bend to ruffle his ears,
And together we walk briskly home.
Perhaps, summer will return?

Gemma North

Time

When I was a girl there was always time,
There was always time to spare.
There was always time to sit in the sun;
And we were never done
With lazing and flirting,
And doing our embroidery,
And keeping up our memory books,
And brushing our hair,
And writing little notes,
And going on picnics,
And dancing, dancing, dancing, dancing –
When I was a girl there was always time to waste.
Thank the Lord.

When I was a young woman there was always time
There was always time to spare.
There was always time to walk in the sun,
And we were never done
With going to weddings,
Our own and our friends,
And going to parties,
Away at weekends,
And having our children
And bringing them up,
And talking, talking, talking, talking –
When I was a young woman there was always time to enjoy
things.
Thank the Lord.

And when I was an elderly woman there was no more time,
There was no more time to spare.
There was no more time to sit in the sun,
For we were never done
With answering the telephone,
And looking at the TV,
And doing baby-sitting,
And talking to our friends,
And shopping, shopping, shopping, shopping,
And washing-up, washing-up, washing-up,
Writing letters, writing letters,
Rushing, rushing, rushing,
And we were always hurried,
And we were never bored.
When I was an elderly woman
There was never time to think.

Thank the Lord.

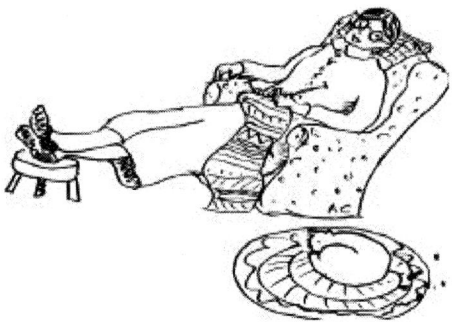

But now I'm an old old woman,
So I want the last word:
There is no such thing as time –
Only this very minute and I'm in it.

Thank the Lord.

Joyce Grenfell
1910 – 1979

Abou Ben Adhem

Abou Ben Adhem (may his tribe increase!)
Awoke one night from a deep dream of peace,
And saw, within the moonlight in his room,
Making it rich, and like a lily in bloom,
An Angel writing in a book of gold:

Exceeding peace had made Ben Adhem bold,
And to the Presence in the room he said,
"What writest thou?" The Vision raised its head,
And with a look made of all sweet accord
Answered, "The names of those who love the Lord."

"And is mine one?" said Abou. "Nay, not so,"
Replied the Angel. Abou spoke more low,
But cheerily still; and said, "I pray thee, then,
Write me as one who loves his fellow men."

The Angel wrote, and vanished. The next night
It came again with a great wakening light,
And showed the names whom love of God had blessed,
And, lo! Ben Adhem's name led all the rest!

Leigh Hunt

1784 – 1859

Angel

Sitting down at the kitchen table sewing
With my lamb on the floor
Making a meal in the room
Sitting by the fire
Chickens pecking at the ground.

A dazzling white
Shining in the distance

Every step towards me a path of happiness
A messenger from heaven

His halo like snow
Gown like frosted glitter
Wings like velvet cushions,
Hair like the sun
His eyes shine like bright stars.

"Mary, you will have a baby and he will be called Jesus"
"I am only a child myself and I'm not even married,
Why did he pick me?"

The angel vanished
Was Mary dreaming?

Rosie Houston Aged 9

From Jennifer Hudson - Radway

Futility

Move him into the sun--
Gently, its touch awoke him once,
At home, whispering of fields unsown.
Always it woke him, even in France,
Until this morning and this snow.
If anything might rouse him now
The kind old sun will know.

Think how it wakes the seeds,--
Woke, once, the clays of a cold star.
Are limbs, so dear-achieved, are sides,
Full-nerved--still warm--too hard to stir?
Was it for this the clay grew tall?
--O what made fatuous sunbeams toil
To break earth's sleep at all?

Wilfred Owen
1893 – 1918

From Sheila Mellor – Warmington

Pied Beauty

Glory be to God for dappled things –
For skies of couple-colour as a brinded cow;
For rose-moles all in stipple upon trout that swim;
Fresh-firecoal chestnut-falls; finches'wings;
Landscape plotted and pieced – fold, fallow and plough;
And all trades, their gear and tackle and trim.

All things counter, original, spare, strange;
Whatever is fickle, freckled (who knows how?)
With swift, slow; sweet, sour; adazzle, dim;
He fathers-forth whose beauty is past change:
Praise him.

Gerard Manley Hopkins
1844- 89

From Cynthia and Roger Bayliss - Warmington

How Do I Love Thee?

How do I love thee? Let me count the ways.
I love thee to the depth and breadth and height
My soul can reach, when feeling out of sight
For the ends of being and ideal grace.
I love thee to the level of every day's
Most quiet need, by sun and candle-light.
I love thee freely, as men strive for right.
I love thee purely, as they turn from praise.
I love thee with the passion put to use
In my old griefs, and with my childhood's faith.
I love thee with a love I seemed to lose
With my lost saints. I love thee with the breath,
Smiles, tears, of all my life; and, if God choose,
I shall but love thee better after death.

Elizabeth Barrett Browning
1806 – 1861

From Richard Neale - Warmington

There's Wisdom in Women

But there's wisdom in women, of more than they have known,
And thoughts go blowing through them, are wiser than their
own.

Rupert Brooke
1887 – 1915

She Walks in Beauty

She walks in beauty, like the night
Of cloudless climes and starry skies;
And all that's best of dark and bright
    Meet in her aspect and her eyes:
Thus mellow'd to that tender light
    Which heaven to gaudy day denies.

One shade the more, one ray the less,
    Had half impair'd the nameless grace
Which waves in every raven tress,
    Or softly lightens o'er her face;
Where thoughts serenely sweet express
        How pure, how dear their dwelling-place.

And on that cheek, and o'er that brow,
    So soft, so calm, yet eloquent,
The smiles that win, the tints that glow,
    But tell of days in goodness spent,
A mind at peace with all below,
    A heart whose love is innocent!

George Gordon Lord Byron
1788-1824

Stop all the clocks

Stop all the clocks, cut off the telephone,
Prevent the dog from barking with a juicy bone,
Silence the pianos and with muffled drum
Bring out the coffin, let the mourners come.

Let aeroplanes circle moaning overhead
Scribbling on the sky the message He Is Dead,
Put crêpe bows round the white necks of the public doves,
Let the traffic policemen wear black cotton gloves.

He was my North, my South, my East and West,
My working week and my Sunday rest,
My noon, my midnight, my talk, my song;
I thought that love would last for ever: I was wrong.

The stars are not wanted now: put out every one;
Pack up the moon and dismantle the sun;
Pour away the ocean and sweep up the wood.
For nothing now can ever come to any good.

WH Auden
1907 – 1973

The Donkey

When fishes flew and forest walked
And figs grew upon thorn,
Some moment when the moon was blood
Then surely I was born.

With monstrous head and sickening cry
And ears like errant wings,
The devil's walking parody
On all four-footed things.

The tattered outlaw of the earth,
Of ancient crooked will;
Starve, scourge, deride me: I am dumb,
I keep my secret still.

Fools! For I also had my hour;
One far fierce hour and sweet:
There was a shout about my ears,
And palms before my feet.

G. K. Chesterton
1874-1936

Candle Power

Candles
Glow softly,
Lighting the rooms
With flickering, pulsating shadows.
Light surrounding deep dark chasms,
Changing the familiar into unknown mystery.
No more humming from our domestic appliances
No telly – no technology – no buzzing
The power lines are down,
We're happily transported
Dark Age
Again.

Jennie Boyle

Re-Generations

I have a niece, one year and one month old.
I had a father, whose home now grows cold.
Sixty-four years, and more than half with me,
The first man that I loved: will always be.

The day she came, a mad motorway drive
Brought me to her, so small and so alive.
That same black tarmac, later in the year
Connected only grief, and pain, and fear.

My brother-father, tight with love and pride,
As brother-son bereaved, had loved, and cried.
When newly-orphaned, she, held in our arm,
Gave to our jangled nerves, innocent balm.

And by some mystery, ancient healing skill
She gave new purpose, re-awakening will.
By love created, so love she creates;
From winter's depths, spring shoots re-generates.

In cold December, we could barely cope;
Her nine months life gave warmth, comfort and hope.
I have a niece, whose life is sharp and new.
Her grandfather, who loved us, loved her too.

Shona Walton

Remember

Remember me when I am gone away,
Gone far away into the silent land;
When you can no more hold me by the hand,
Nor I half turn to go, yet turning stay.
Remember me when no more day by day
You tell me of our future that you planned:
Only remember me; you understand
It will be late to counsel then or pray.
Yet if you should forget me for a while
And afterwards remember, do not grieve:
For if the darkness and corruption leave
A vestige of the thoughts that once I had,
Better by far you should forget and smile
Than that you should remember and be sad.

Christina Georgina Rossetti
1830–1894

From Brian Russell – Radway

Life a Duty

I slept and dreamed that life was Beauty;
I woke and found that life was Duty.
Was thy dream then a shadowy lie?
Toil on, poor heart, unceasingly;
And thou shalt find they dream to be
A truth and noonday light to thee.

Ellen Hooper
1816-1841

Love

Love is a great thing,
Yea, a great and thorough good;
For it carries a burden that is no burden,
And makes everything that is bitter, sweet and savoury
Nothing is sweeter than love,
Nothing more courageous,
Nothing fuller or better in heaven and earth;
Because love is born of God.
He that loveth, flieth, runneth and rejoiceth,
He is free, and cannot be held in.

Love feels no burden, thinks nothing of trouble,
Attempts what is above its strength,
Thinks nothing impossible.
Though weary, love is not tired;
Though alarmed, it is not confounded;
But as a lively flame and burning torch,
It forces its way upwards,
And securely passes through all.

Thomas a. Kempis
1380 – 1471

Cumulus

Ploughed and tilled by the wind;
Like furrows in a field scoring lines across the sky
Or an ephemeral shroud suspended on high.
Different phases of a symphony waiting to begin –
'Alto' moving to 'cirr', subtly shifting before the eye.

Occasional contrails like the tail of a kite,
A brief interlude; a sudden slash of blue
Patched over again and obscured from view.
New forms take shape in the changing light;
Latin stems coming through –

Staccato phrases, dancing detached –
The accent on cirrus; a curl of hair
Born quickly away on the allegro air.
Then a slight dissonance as the cadence catches;
And the rhythms of the stratus begin to slur.

Into a legato, leisurely lethargic
In its slow-moving pace,
Building and billowing with majestic grace,
While melancholy mammatus; pouch-like sacks in sinking air
Ensemble together in the pregnant space.

Tania Adams
June 2004

From Bill Voisey – Upton

If I should go before the rest of you

If I should go before the rest of you
Break not a flower nor inscribe a stone,
Nor, when I'm gone, speak of me in a Sunday voice,
But be your usual selves that I have known.

Weep if you must. Parting is hell,
But life goes on – so sing as well.

Joyce Grenfell
1910 – 1979

From Robert Cook - Ratley

Thoughts

To plant a garden for a friend
Is to hope that friendships never end
And to make a garden of my thoughts and dreams
Becomes not so easy if dreams become reality
And such a course pursued may create fatality
But should we meet, let's not despise
But see past pleasures in our eyes
For we would know, who know the truth
That time once stood still beneath this heavenly roof.

Anon

From Luise Gunter and Gemma North – Shotteswell
Christopher Lamb – Warmington

High Flight

Oh, I have slipped the surly bonds of earth
And danced the skies on laughter-silvered wings
Sunward I have climbed, and joined the tumbling mirth
Of sun-split clouds –
And done a hundred things
You have not dreamed of – wheeled and soared and swung
High in the sunlit silence. Hov'ring there,
I've chased the shouting wind along, and flung
My eager craft through footless halls of air.
Up, up the long, delirious, burning blue
I've topped the wind-swept heights with easy grace
Where never lark or even eagle flew –
And, while with silent lifting mind I've trod
The high untrespassed sanctity of space,
Put out my hand and touched the face of God.

John Gillespie Magee
1922-1941

R.Tatchell.

From Janet Neale – Warmington
Abby Symons and Matt Duncan – Ratley

If

If you can keep your head when all about you
Are losing theirs and blaming it on you,
If you can trust yourself when all men doubt you
But make allowance for their doubting too,
If you can wait and not be tired by waiting,
Or being lied about, don't deal in lies,
Or being hated, don't give way to hating,
And yet don't look too good, nor talk too wise:

If you can dream – and not make dreams your master,
If you can think – and not make thoughts your aim;
If you can meet with Triumph and Disaster
And treat those two impostors just the same;
If you can bear to hear the truth you've spoken
Twisted by knaves to make a trap for fools,
Or watch the things you gave your life to, broken,
And stoop and build 'em up with worn-out tools:

If you can make one heap of all your winnings
And risk it all on one turn of pitch-and-toss,
And lose, and start again at your beginnings
And never breath a word about your loss:
If you can force your heart and nerve and sinew
To serve your turn long after they are gone,
And so hold on when there is nothing in you
Except the Will which says to them: "Hold on!"

If you can talk with crowds and keep your virtue,
Or walk with kings – nor lose the common touch,
If neither foes nor loving friends can hurt you:
If all men count with you, but none too much,.
If you can fill the unforgiving minute
With sixty seconds' worth of distance run,
Yours is the Earth and everything that's in it,
And – which is more – you'll be a Man, my son!

Rudyard Kipling
1865-1936

From Tina Lamb –Warmington

The Kingdom

It's a long way off but inside it
There are quite different things going on:
Festivals at which the poor man
Is king and the consumptive is
Healed: mirrors in which the blind look
At themselves and love looks at them
Back; and industry is for mending
The bent bones and the minds fractured
By life. It's a long way off, but to get
There takes no time and admission
Is free, if you will purge yourself
Of desire, and present yourself with
Your need only and the simple offering
Of your faith, green as a leaf.

R.S.Thomas
1913-2000

From George Adams – Warmington

Indian Prayer

When I am dead
Cry for me a little,
Think of me sometimes,
But not too much.
Think of me now and again
As I was in life
At some moments it's pleasant to recall,
But not for long.
Leave me in peace,
And I shall leave you in peace,
And while you live
Let your thoughts be with the living.

Traditional

From Pat Thomas, Jay Williams – Warmington,
Clare Brown, Patricia Orr – Ratley

Journey of the Magi

A cold coming we had of it,
Just the worst time of the year
For a journey and such a long journey:
The ways deep and the weather sharp,
The very dead of winter.
And the camels galled, sore-footed, refractory,
Lying down in the melted snow.
There were times when we regretted
The summer palaces on slopes, the terraces,
And the silken girls bringing sherbet.
Then the camel men cursing and grumbling
And running away, and wanting their liquor and women,
And the night-fires going out, and the lack of shelters,
And the cities dirty and the towns unfriendly
And the villages dirty and charging high prices:
A hard time we had of it.
At the end we preferred to travel all night,
Sleeping in snatches,
With the voices singing in our ears, saying
That this was all folly.

Then at dawn we came down to a temperate valley,
Wet, below the snow line, smelling of vegetation;
With a running stream and a water mill beating the darkness,
And three trees on the low sky,
And an old white horse galloped away in the meadow.
Then we came to a tavern with vine-leaves over the lintel,
Six hands at an open door dicing for pieces of silver,
And feet kicking the empty wineskins.
But there was no information and so we continued
And arrived at evening, not a moment too soon
Finding the place; it was (you may say) satisfactory.

All this was a long time ago, I remember,
And I would do it again, but set down
This: were we led all that way for
Birth or Death? There was a Birth, certainly,
We had evidence and no doubt. I had seen birth and death,
But had thought they were different: this Birth was
Hard and bitter agony for us, like Death, our death.
We returned to our places, these Kingdoms,
But no longer at ease here, in the old dispensation,
With an alien people clutching their gods.
I should be glad of another death.

T.S. Eliot
1888-1965

From Jay Williams – Warmington

D.S.W.

Yesterday the snow fell
And I thought of you.

I watched from the window as it came in furious haste,
Impatient to touch the naked earth,
And I thought of you.

The trees moved with the onslaught,
Their limbs outstretched as if to catch elusive swansdown,
And I thought of you.

Today the snow is soft and silent,
Transforming the earth into a virgin bed, deep and soporific,
And I think of you.

I am walking in the snow and I think of you.
I mar its maiden freshness with my boots but I tread gently,
Thinking of you.

J.W.
Warmington 1990

The Destruction of Sennacharib

The Assyrian came down like the wolf on the fold,
And his cohorts were gleaming in purple and gold;
And the sheen of their spears was like stars on the sea,
When the blue wave rolls nightly on deep Galilee.

Like the leaves of the forest when Summer is green,
That host with their banners at sunset were seen:
Like the leaves of the forest when Autumn hath blown,
That host on the morrow lay withered and strown.

For the Angel of Death spread his wings on the blast,
And breathed in the face of the foe as he passed;
And the eyes of the sleepers waxed deadly and chill,
And their hearts but once heaved, and for ever grew still!

And there lay the steed with his nostril all wide,
But through it there rolled not the breath of his pride;
And the foam of his gasping lay white on the turf,
And cold as the spray of the rock-beating surf.

And there lay the rider distorted and pale,
With the dew on his brow, and the rust on his mail:
And the tents were all silent, the banners alone,
The lances unlifted, the trumpet unblown.

And the widows of Ashur are loud in their wail,
And the idols are broke in the temple of Baal;
And the might of the Gentile, unsmote by the sword,
Hath melted like snow in the glance of the Lord!

George Gordon, Lord Byron
1788 – 1824

Butterflies in Church

Butterfly, butterfly, why come you here?
This is no place for you.
Go sip the honey-dew sweet and clear
Or bathe in the morning dew.

This is the place to think of heaven,
This is the place to pray.
You have no sins to be forgiven.
Butterfly, go away!

**William Cowper
1731 – 1800**

Your Garden

I close my eyes and find myself in Your garden,
And it is breathtaking, O, it's a beautiful place.
Before me lies the mystery of Your garden
Reaching eternally endlessly into space.
There dwells serenity and peace among the flowers,
There in the shade of leafy trees after the showers
I breathe the fragrance in the air of saintly prayer.

You beckon me, my Lord, my friend and my master,
You call me to worship, call me to come and adore,
And cause me to see with lightning speed – only faster
Your waiting, Your longing, Your pain for my sin You bore.
With timeless graces You lift the head of every flower
And turn their faces to see Your power
And keep their sight upon Your light.

I hear the sound of distant music and singing
Though it is vibrant, yet it is gentle and discreet
And all around, what seems like laughter ringing
Peals into symphonies and melodies so sweet.
My heart it knows it must expand, it's raised so much
It hears the call of his demand and feels his touch
With urgency as ne'er before to love Him more.

What joy there is! It is beyond all sense and reason,
Beyond the understanding and knowledge of the mind.
O to be His – to live the "true life" season,
To grow in Him – life of the highest kind –
O, here lies paradise indeed, garden of Glory,
Ministering to my deepest need, He writes His story
Upon my heart that I shall know he loves me so.

Karin Castle

Don't Give Up

When things go wrong as they sometimes will,
When the road you're trudging seems all uphill,
When the funds are low and the debts are high,
And you want to smile but you have to sigh,
When care is pressing you down a bit,
Rest if you must, but don't you quit.
Life is queer with its twists and turns,
As everyone of us sometimes learns,
And many a failure turns about,
When you might have won had you stuck it out.
Don't give up if the pace seems slow,
You may succeed with another blow.
Success is failure turned inside out ,
The silver tint of the cloud of doubt;
And you never can tell how close you are,
It may be near when it seems so far.
So stick to the fight when you're hardest hit,
It's when things seem worst YOU MUST NOT QUIT.

Author unknown

For Johnny

Do not despair
For Johnny head-in-air,
He sleeps as sound
As Johnny underground.

Fetch out no shroud
For Johnny in-the-cloud,
And keep your tears
For him in after years.

Better by far
For Johnny the-bright-star,
To keep your head,
And see his children fed.

John Pudney
1906-1977

Metamorphoses

Then sprang up first the Golden Age, which of itself
maintained
The truth and right of everything, unforced and unconstrained.
There was no fear of punishment, there was no threatening
law
In brazen tables nailed up to keep the folks in awe.
There was no man would crouch and creep to Judge with cap
in hand;
They lived safe without a Judge in every realm and land.
The lofty pine tree was not hewn from mountains where it
stood,
In seeking strange and foreign lands, to rove upon the flood.
Man knew no other countries yet than where themselves did
keep:
There was town enclosed yet with walls and ditches deep.
No horn or trumpet was in use, no sword or helmet worn;
The world was such that soldiers' help might easily be forborn.
The fertile earth as yet was free, untouched of sword or
plough,
And yet it yielded of itself of everything enough.

Ovid 43 BC – 18 AD
Translated by Arthur Golding 1536 - 1605

Little Gidding

With the drawing of this Love and the voice of this Calling

We shall not cease from exploration
And the end of all our exploring
Will be to arrive where we started
And know the place for the first time.
Through the unknown, remembered gate
When the last of earth left to discover
Is that which was the beginning;
At the source of the longest river
The voice of the hidden waterfall
And the children in the apple-tree
Not known, because not looked for
But heard, half-heard, in the stillness
Between two waves of the sea.
Quick now, here, now, always –
A condition of complete simplicity
(Costing not less than everything)
And all shall be well and
All manner of thing shall be well
When the tongues of flame are in-folded
Into the crowned knot of fire
And the fire and the rose are one.

T.S. Eliot
1888 - 1965

"On a Fly drinking out of his Cup"

Busy, curious, thirsty fly!
Drink with me and drink as I:
Feely welcome to my cup,
Couldst thou sip and sip it up:
Make the most of life you may,
Life is short and wears away.

Both alike are mine and thine
Hastening quick to their decline:
Thine's a summer, mine's no more,
Though repeated to threescore.
Threescore summers, when they're gone,
Will appear as short as one!

William Oldys
1696-1761

BILL RICHARDSON

From Clare Brown and Patricia Orr - Ratley

Do Not Go Gentle into That Good Night

Do not go gentle into that good night,
Old age should burn and rave at close of day;
Rage, rage against the dying of the light.

Though wise men at their end know dark is right,
Because their words had forked no lightning they
Do not go gentle into that good night.

Good men, the last wave by, crying how bright
Their frail deeds might have danced in a green bay,
Rage, rage against the dying of the light.

Wild men who caught and sang the sun in flight,
And learn, too late, they grieved it on its way,
Do not go gentle into that good night.

Grave men, near death, who see with blinding sight
Blind eyes could blaze like meteors and be gay,
Rage, rage against the dying of the light.

And you, my father, there on the sad height,
Curse, bless, me now with your fierce tears, I pray.
Do not go gentle into that good night.
Rage, rage against the dying of the light.

Dylan Thomas
1914 – 1953

Morning

Did the sun shine that morning
When the tumultuous night gave way to daylight?
Were the clouds held back,
So the clear skies that had opened before stars and angel
choirs
Were the gateway for the brightness of day?
After the chaos of travellers crowding in,
The confusion of the hastening, excited shepherds
Bursting through the door,
Was the clear calm light like a blessing,
A pause for refreshment before moving on with the
Flow of the day's demands?
Did it seem as if, for a moment,
The peace of heaven, which is beyond understanding,
Rested upon them,
Calmed and cloaked them,
Lifted eyes and minds above the everyday, the here-and-now,
Towards the eternal infinity that is God,

Because God was among them?

Andrea Harding-Smith
23 November 2002

Leaving the Tate

Coming out with your clutch of postcards
In a Tate Gallery bag and another clutch
Of images packed into your head you pause
On the steps to look across the river

And there's a new one: light bright buildings
A streak of brown water, and such a sky
You wonder who painted it – Constable? No:
Too brilliant. Crome? No: too ecstatic -

A madly pure Pre-Raphaelite sky,
Perhaps, sheer blue apart from the white plumes
Rushing up it (today, that is,
April. Another day would be different

But it wouldn't matter. All skies work)
Cut to the lower right for a detail:
Seagulls pecking on mud, below
Two office blocks and a Georgian terrace

Now swing to the left, and take in plane-trees
Bobbled with seeds, and that brick building,
And a red bus… Cut it off just there,
By the lamp-post. Leave the scaffolding in.

That's you next one. Curious how
These outdoor pictures didn't exist
Before you'd looked at the indoor pictures,
The ones on the walls. But here they are no,

Marching out of their panorama
And queuing up for the viewfinder
Your eye's become. You can isolate them
By holding you optic muscles still.

You can zoom in on figure studies
(that boy with the rucksack), or still lives,
Abstracts, townscapes. No one made them.
The light painted them. You're in charge

Of the hanging committee. Put what space
You like around the one you fix on,
And gloat. Art multiplies itself.
Art's whatever you choose to frame.

Fleur Adcock b.1934

Desiderata

Go placidly amid the noise and haste and remember what
peace there may be in silence.
As far as possible, without surrender, be on good terms with
all persons.
Speak your truth quietly and clearly: and listen to others,
Even to the dull and ignorant; they too have their story.

Avoid loud and aggressive persons; they are vexations to the
spirit.
If you compare yourself with others, you may become vain
and bitter,
For always there will be greater and lesser persons than
yourself.
Enjoy your achievements as well as your plans.

Keep interested in your own career, however humble;
It is a real possession in the changing fortunes of time.
Exercise caution in your business affairs, for the world is full of
trickery.
But let this not blind you to what virtue there is;
Many persons strive for high ideals, and everywhere life is full
of heroism.

Be yourself. Especially do not feign affection. Neither be
cynical about love;
For in the face of aridity and disenchantment it is as perennial
as the grass.
Take kindly the counsel of the years, gracefully surrendering
the things of youth.
Nurture strength of spirit to shield you in sudden misfortune.
But do not distress yourself with dark imaginings.
Many fears are born of fatigue and loneliness.

Beyond a wholesome discipline, be gentle with yourself.
You are a child of the universe no less than the trees and the stars;
You have a right to be here. And whether or not it is clear to you,
No doubt the universe is unfolding as it should.

Therefore be at peace with God, whatever you conceive Him to be.
And whatever your labours and aspirations, in the noisy confusion of life, keep peace with your soul.
With all its shame, drudgery and broken dreams, it is still a beautiful world.
Be cheerful. Strive to be happy.

Max Ehrmann
1812 - 1945

From Liz Newman - Warmington

Death, be not Proud

Death, be not proud, though some have called thee
Mighty and dreadful, for, thou art not so,
For, those, whom thou think'st, thou dost overthrow,
Die not, poor Death, not yet canst thou kill me.
From rest and sleep, which but thy pictures be,
Much pleasure, then from thee, much more must flow,
And soonest our best men with thee do go,
Rest of their bones, and soul's delivery.
Though art slave to fate, chance, kings, and desperate men.
And dost with poison, war, and sickness dwell;
And poppy or charms can make us sleep as well,
And better than thy stroke; why swell'st thou then?
One short sleep past, we wake eternally,
    And death shall be no more; death, though shalt die.

John Donne
1572-1631

Dark Stuff

Putting off the evil moment,
Inertia like an illness
Poetic paralysis
Dredging up thoughts only to dismiss
Them back down into the dark abyss
Waiting while they soften
Then sink slowly into the sediment;
Murky metamorphosis.
Dark, shifting forces stir up the silt;
A bitter brew.
Like watching the black stuff settle
In a glass on the bar;
Down-drafts of creative clouds,
Anticipation tangible,
Until the perfect finish line comes into view.

Tania Adams
June 2004

From Joan and Tony Thomas and Jennie Boyle – Warmington
Frances Freer - Radway

The Tyger

Tyger, tyger, burning bright
In the forests of the night,
What immortal hand or eye
Could frame thy fearful symmetry?

In what distant deeps or skies
Burnt the fire of thine eyes?
On what wings dare he aspire?
What the hand dare seize the fire?

And what shoulder and what art,
Could twist the sinews of thy heart?
And when thy heart began to beat,
What dread hand and what dread feet?

What the hammer? what the chain?
In what furnace was thy brain?
What the anvil? What dread grasp
Dare its deadly terrors clasp?

When the stars threw down their spears,
And water'd heaven with their tears,
Did He smile His work to see?
Did He who made the lamb make thee?

Tyger, tyger, burning bright
In the forests of the night,
What immortal hand or eye
Dare frame thy fearful symmetry?

William Blake
1757–1827

R. Tatchell.

53

An Irish Airman Foresees His Death

I know that I shall meet my fate
Somewhere among the clouds above;
Those that I fight I do not hate,
Those that I guard I do not love;
My country is Kiltartan Cross,
My countrymen Kiltartan's poor,
No likely end could bring them loss
Or leave them happier than before.
Nor law, nor duty bade me fight,
Nor public men, nor cheering crowds,
A lonely impulse of delight
Drove to this tumult in the clouds;
I balanced all, brought all to mind,
The years to come seemed waste of breath,
A waste of breath the years behind
In balance with this life, this death.

William Butler Yeats (1865-1939)

Dulce et Decorum est

Bent double, like old beggars under sacks,
Knock-kneed, coughing like hags, we cursed through sludge,
Till on the haunting flares we turned out backs,
And towards our distant rest began to trudge.
Men marched asleep. Many had lost their boots,
But limped on, blood-shod. All went lame, all blind;
Drunk with fatigue; deaf even to the hoots

Of gas-shells dropping softly behind.

Gas! GAS! Quick, boys!--An ecstasy of fumbling
Fitting the clumsy helmets just in time,
But someone still was yelling out and stumbling
And flound'ring like a man in fire or lime.--
Dim through the misty panes and thick green light,
As under a green sea, I saw him drowning.

In all my dreams before my helpless sight
He plunges at me, guttering, choking, drowning.

If in some smothering dreams, you too could pace
Behind the wagon that we flung him in,
And watch the white eyes writhing in his face,
His hanging face, like a devil's sick of sin,
If you could hear, at every jolt, the blood
Come gargling from the froth-corrupted lungs
Bitter as the cud
Of vile, incurable sores on innocent tongues,--
My friend, you would not tell with such high zest
To children ardent for some desperate glory,
The old Lie: Dulce et decorum est
Pro patria mori

Wilfred Owen

1893 – 1918

The Highwayman

Part I

The wind was a torrent of darkness among the gusty trees,
The moon was a ghostly galleon tossed upon cloudy seas,
The road was a ribbon of moonlight, over the purple moor,
And the highwayman came riding-
   Riding-riding-
The highwayman came riding, up to the old inn-door.

He'd a French cocked-hat on his forehead, a bunch of lace at
his chin,
A coat of the claret velvet, and breeches of brown doe-skin;
They fitted with never a wrinkle: his boots were up to the thigh!
And he rode with a jewelled twinkle,
   His pistol butts a-twinkle,
His rapier hilt a-twinkle, under the jewelled sky.

Over the cobbles he clattered and clashed in the dark inn-
yard,
And he tapped with his whip on the shutters, but all was
locked and barred;
He whistled a tune to the window, and who should be waiting
there
But the landlord's black-eyed daughter,
   Bess, the landlord's daughter,
Plaiting a dark red love-knot into her long black hair.

And dark in the old inn-yard a stable-wicket creaked
Where Tim the ostler listened; his face was white and peaked;
His eyes were hollows of madness, his hair like mouldy hay,
But he loved the landlord's daughter,
   The landlord's red-lipped daughter,
Dumb as a dog he listened, and he heard the robber say-

"One kiss, my bonny sweetheart, I'm after a prize to-night,
But I shall be back with the yellow gold before the morning light;
Yet, if they press me sharply, and harry me through the day,
Then look for me by moonlight,
            Watch for me by moonlight,
I'll come to thee by moonlight, though hell should bar the way."

He rose upright in the stirrups; he scarce could reach her hand,
But she loosened her hair i' the casement! His face burnt like a brand
As the black cascade of perfume came tumbling over his breast;
And he kissed its waves in the moonlight,
            (Oh, sweet black waves in the moonlight!)
Then he tugged at his rein in the moonlight, and galloped away to the West.

Part II

He did not come in the dawning; he did not come at noon;
And out o' the tawny sunset, before the rise o' the moon,
When the road was a gipsy's ribbon, looping the purple moor,
A red-coat troop came marching-
            Marching-marching-
King George's men came marching, up to the old inn-door.

They said no word to the landlord, they drank his ale instead,
But they gagged his daughter and bound her to the foot of her narrow bed;
Two of them knelt at her casement, with muskets at their side!
There was death at every window;
            And hell at one dark window;
For Bess could see, through the casement, the road that *he* would ride.

They had tied her up to attention, with many a sniggering jest;
They bound a musket beside her, with the barrel beneath her
breast!
"Now keep good watch!" and they kissed her.
        She heard the dead man say-
Look for me by moonlight;
        Watch for me by moonlight;
I'll come to thee by moonlight, though hell should bar the way!

She twisted her hands behind her; but all the knots held good!
She writhed her hands till here fingers were wet with sweat or
blood!
They stretched and strained in the darkness, and the hours
crawled by like years,
Till, now, on the stroke of midnight,
        Cold, on the stroke of midnight,
The tip of one finger touched it! The trigger at least was hers!

The tip of one finger touched it;she strove no more for the rest!
Up, she stood up to attention, with the barrel beneath her
breast,
She would not risk their hearing; she would not strive again;
For the road lay bare in the moonlight;
        Blank and bare in the moonlight;
And the blood of her veins in the moonlight throbbed to her
love's refrain.

Tlot-tlot; tlot-tlot! Had they heard it? The horse-hoofs
ringing clear;
Tlot-tlot, tlot-tlot, in the distance? Were they deaf that they did
not hear?
Down the ribbon of moonlight, over the brow of the hill,
The highwayman came riding,
        Riding, riding!
The red-coats looked to their priming! She stood strait and still!

Tlot-tlot, in the frosty silence! *Tlot-tlot*, in the echoing night!
Nearer he came and nearer! Her face was like a light!
Her eyes grew wide for a moment; she drew one last deep
breath,
Then her finger moved in the moonlight,
        Her musket shattered the moonlight,
Shattered her breast in the moonlight and warned him-with her
death.

He turned; he spurred to the West; he did not know who stood
Bowed, with her head o'er the musket, drenched with her own
red blood!
Not till the dawn he heard it, his face grew grey to hear
How Bess, the landlord's daughter,
       The landlord's black-eyed daughter,
Had watched for her love in the moonlight, and died in the
darkness there.

Back, he spurred like a madman, shrieking a curse to the sky,
With the white road smoking behind him and his rapier
brandished high!
Blood-red were his spurs i' the golden noon; wine-red was his
velvet coat,
When they shot him down on the highway,
       Down like a dog on the highway,
And he lay in his blood on the highway, with a bunch of lace at
his throat.

*And still of a winter's night, they say, when the wind is in the
trees,*
When the moon is a ghostly galleon tossed upon cloudy seas,
When the road is a ribbon of moonlight over the purple moor,
A highwayman comes riding-
       Riding-riding-
A highwayman comes riding, up to the old inn-door.

Over the cobbles he clatters and clangs in the dark inn-yard,
*And he taps with his whip on the shutters, but all is locked and
barred;*
*He whistles a tune to the window, and who should be waiting
there*
But the landlord's black-eyed daughter,
       Bess, the landlord's daughter,
Plaiting a dark red love-knot into her long black hair.

Alfred Noyes
1880 – 1958

Not Waving but Drowning

Nobody heard him, the dead man
But still he lay moaning:
I was much further out than you thought
And not waving but drowning.

Poor chap, he always loved larking
And now he's dead
It must have been too cold for him his heart gave way,
They said.

Oh, no, no no, it was too cold always
(Still the dead one lay moaning)
I was much too far out all my life
And not waving but drowning.

Stevie Smith. 1903 – 1971

CUCKOO

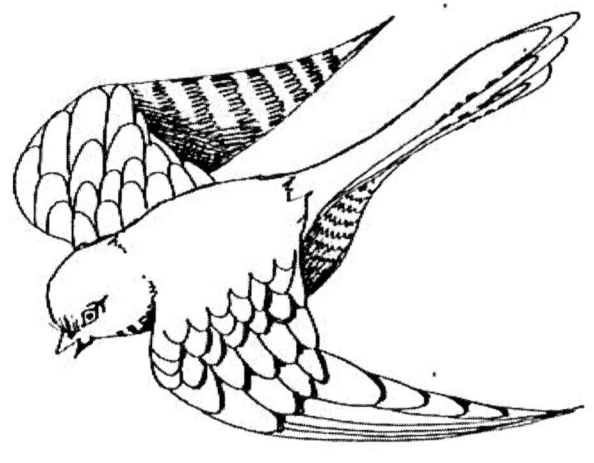

How to avoid kissing your parents in Public

RUN FOR IT at the first sign of parent puckering.

SMILE, look as if you don't mind and then say you feel really sick.

WHIRL AROUND very fast and go, Mwah, Mwah!
so that they think they got you when in fact they missed.

DUCK so that the kiss lands just above your head.

ASK them to put it in your pocket before you get to
school so that you can save it for later when nobody's looking.

NEVER clean your teeth and they won't want to
  Or:
DEMAND GARLIC with every meal and they wont want to
either.

SAY you're doing a sponsored 'no kissing competition' and
donate ten pence to charity for every missed kiss..(Note: This
could prove to be expensive.)

TURN INTO A FROG. (Only resort to this if your mum doesn't
believe in fairy tales.

IF ALL ELSE FAILS, cling to their legs and beg them to give
you a million sloppy kisses. They'll be so worried that they'll
either take you to the doctor...
  Or:

    NEVER KISS YOU IN PUBLIC AGAIN!

Lindsey Macrae
b.1961

Excuses for Drinking

Some drink to make them wide awake,
And some to make them sleep;
Some drink because they merry are,
And some drink because they weep.

Some drink because they're very hot,
And some because they're cold;
Some drink to cheer them when they're young,
And some because they're old.

Some drink to give them appetite,
And some to aid digestion;
Some, for the doctor says it's right,
And some without question.

Some drink when they a bargain make,
And some because of loss;
Some drink when they their pleasure take,
And some when they are cross.

Some drink for sake of company,
While some drink on the sly;
And many drink but never think
About the reason why.

From *Nuts to crack for Moderate Drinkers*

J. Milton Smith
1890

Be Impolite

Don't waste your smile
On a crocodile,
For though his grin is wide
You will find
What's on his mind is,
"Will you come inside?"

Michael Dugan

Cat Kisses

Sandpaper kisses
On the cheek or chin
That is a way for the day to begin!

Sandpaper kisses
A cuddle, a purr
I have an alarm clock
That's covered with fur.

Bobbie Katz (1933 -)

Loss

The day he moved out was terrible –
That evening she went through hell
His absence wasn't a problem
But the corkscrew had gone as well.

Wendy Cope
b.1945

Hug

It's funny how a little hug
Makes everyone feel good;
In every place and language
It's always understood.
Hugs don't need new equipment,
Special batteries, or parts;
Just open up your arms,
And open up your hearts.

Anon

Warning

When I am an old woman I shall wear purple
With a red hat which doesn't go, and doesn't suit me,
And I shall spend my pension on brandy and summer gloves
And satin sandals, and say we've no money for butter.
I shall sit down on the pavement when I'm tired
And gobble up samples in shops and press alarm bells
And run my stick along the public railings
And make up for the sobriety of my youth
I shall go out in my slipper in the rain
And pick flowers in other people's gardens
And learn to spit.

You can wear terrible shirts and grow more fat
And eat three pound of sausages at one go
Or only bread and pickle for a week
And hoard pens and pencils and beer mats and things in
boxes.

But now we must have clothes that keep us dry
And pay our rent and not swear in the street
And set a good example for the children.
We must have friends to dinner and read the papers.

But maybe I ought to practise a little now?
So people who know are not too shocked and surprised
When suddenly I am old, and start to wear purple.

Jenny Joseph
b.1932

Headmaster's Hymn

When a knight won his spurs
In the stories of old,
He was – *'Face the front, David Briggs,*
What have you been told?'
With a shield on this arm
And a lance in his – *'Hey!*
Is that a ball I can see?
Put – it – away.'

No charger have I
And –*'No talking back there.*
You're supposed to be singing,
Not combing your hair.'
Through back into storyland

Giants have – *'Roy,*
This isn't the playground
Stop pushing that boy!'

Let faith be my shield
And – *'Who's eating sweets here*
I'm ashamed of you, Marion
It's not like you dear.'
And let me set free

With – *'Please stop that, Paul King.*
This is no place for whistlers,
We'd rather you sing!'

Allan Ahlberg 1938

How to get on in Society

Phone for the fish knives, Norman
As cook is a little unnerved;
Your kiddies have crumpled the
serviettes
And I must have things daintily served.

Are the requisites all in the toilet?
The frills round the cutlets can wait.
Till the girl has replenished the cruets
And switched on the logs in the grate.

It's ever so close in the lounge dear,
But the vestibule's comfy for tea
And Howard is riding on horseback,
So do come and take some with me.

Now here is a fork for your pastries
And do use the couch for your feet;
I know that I wanted to ask you -
Is trifle sufficient for sweet?

Milk and then just as it comes dear?
I'm afraid the preserve's full of stones;
Beg pardon, I'm soiling the doileys
With afternoon tea-cakes and scones.

John Betjeman
1906-1984

From Mark Sloan – Radway

Mark wrote: *"This sums up Robert Frost for me!"*

Untitled

Forgive, O Lord, my little jokes on Thee
And I'll forgive Thy great big one on me.

Robert Frost
1874 – 1963

ֆֆֆֆ

From Jennie Boyle –Warmington

I love

I love the English country scene
But sometimes think there's too much hookers green,
Especially in august, when the flowers might have lent a
Lightness, don't; being gamboges or magenta.

Stevie Smith
1903 – 1971

In Praise of the Potato

(Written for The Independent Writing Competition in 1991)

*Spitalfields fruit and vegetable market had recently moved
from its original site after 300 years of trading. Competitors
were invited to write a poem honouring a fruit or vegetable.*

In all the years at Spitalfields
The spud to none its status yields.
Remember, when this veg you boil,
That every Brit adores a Royal.
Consider, as you lift your fork,
You may consume the Duke of York,
Or you might shortly swallow down
King Edward or a Pentland Crown.
If to the military you're partial
Home Guard can offer food more martial.
While Pentland Javelin can fight
Slugs, wireworm, scab and even blight.
Should you prefer something more tender,
View the delights of female gender:
Desiree with her flesh pale yellow,
Can please the most demanding fellow.
And Catriona's shallow eyed,
A heavy cropper, best when fried.
Do you prefer a Highland sound?
Then Maris Piper, smooth and round,
With tender tubers, sautéed, creamed,
Will satisfy all you have dreamed.
Baked, mashed or chipped, served with a roast,
Whichever way you like them most,
To praise these rhizomes of our nation,
Raise your glass! Drink a potation!

Creepy-Crawlies

If you happen to have an ant in your pants,
A fly in your eye or a flea,
Don't get in a state, there's nothing to hate
They're beautiful creatures like me.

They live in this land, and just as God planned,
They all have a task to get through,
With young ones to rear, you've nothing to fear,
They're beautiful people like you.

They're here for a reason, and change every season,
Feeding the birds on the lawn,
And birds for their part, all feathers and heart,
Will wake you up early each morn.

But if you despise those horrible flies,
That tickle your nose when asleep,
Just see that your lips are tighter than zips,
Or into your mouth they might creep.

And next time you see a wasp or a bee,
Don't swat him, shout 'got him' and run.
Just leave him alone, he's fine on his own,
Or maybe he'll sting you for fun.

If you're troubles with fleas, just treat them with ease,
Don't wish you were blooming well dead.
Biologic control is good for your soul,
Just sleep with a spider in bed.

When the weather is fine, and ants form a line,
And start to depart with your dinner,
Just watch them go past, it's a good chance to fast,
And maybe you'll grow a bit thinner.

If a wasp or a bee falls into your tea,
And you can't close the teapot much tighter,
Don't give it much thought, just be a good sport,
And rescue the poor little blighter.

Should termites invade the home that you've made,
Remember the reason they do it,
And try to be kind, if one day you find
They've thanked you by chewing right through it.

When cockroaches roam through your family home,
Don't panic, just do what I say.
Remember with love, the Lord up above,
And say to each other: let's pray. (Let's spray).

John R. Seville
Jane Seville's father.

Celia Celia

When I am sad and weary
When I think all hope has gone
When I walk along High Holborn
I think of you with nothing on.

Adrian Mitchell (b.1932)

To Someone who insisted I look up Someone

I rang them up while touring Timbuktu,
Those bosom chums of yours to whom
you're known as *'Who?'*

XJ Kennedy

The Vulture

The vulture eats between his meals;
And that's the reason why
He very rarely feels
As well as you or I.
His eye is dull, his head is bald,
His neck is growing thinner.
So that's a lesson for us all
To only eat at dinner.

Anon

From Linda Clark – Shotteswell
John Field – Warmington

On The Ning Nang Nong

On the Ning Nang Nong
Where the Cows go Bong!
And the Monkeys all say Boo!
There's a Nong Nang Ning
Where the trees go Ping!
And the tea pots Jibber Jabber Joo.
On the Nong Ning Nang,
All the mice go Clang!
And you just can't catch 'em when they do!
So it's Ning Nang Nong!
Cows go Bong!
Nong Nang Ning!
Trees go Ping!
Nong Ning Nang!
The mice go Clang!

What a noisy place to belong,
Is the Ning Nang Ning Nang Nong!!

Spike Milligan
1918-2002

Smiling

Smiling is infectious
You catch it like the flu.
When someone smiled at me today
I started smiling too.
I passed around the corner
And someone saw my grin.
When he smiled I realised
I'd passed it on to him.
I thought about the smile
Then recognised its worth.
A simple smile like mine
Could travel round the earth.
So if you feel a smile begin
Don't leave it undetected.
Lets start and epidemic
And get the world infected.

Author Unknown

From Mark Sloan - Radway

In a Glass of Cider

It seemed I was a mite of sediment
That waited at the bottom to ferment
So I could catch a bubble in ascent.
I rode up on one 'til the bubble burst
and when that left me to sink back reversed
I was no worse off than I was at first.
I'd catch another bubble if I waited.
The thing was to get now and then elated.

Mark wrote: *I first heard this when I was 21 and it has been a source of joy (and often comfort) for more than 40 years.*

Robert Frost
1874 – 1963

Macavity: The Mystery Cat

Macavity's a Mystery Cat: he's called the Hidden Paw -
For he's the master criminal who can defy the Law.
He's the bafflement of Scotland Yard, the Flying Squad's
despair:
For when they reach the scene of crime - *Macavity's not there*!

Macavity, Macavity, there's no one like Macavity,
He's broken every human law, he breaks the law of gravity.
His powers of levitation would make a fakir stare,
And when you reach the scene of crime - *Macavity's not there*!
You may seek him in the basement, you may look up in the air
But I tell you once and once again, *Macavity's not there*!

Mcavity's a ginger cat, he's very tall and thin;
You would know him if you saw him, for his eyes are sunken
in.
His brow is deeply lined with thought, his head is highly
domed;
His coat is dusty from neglect, his whiskers are uncombed.
He sways his head from side to side, with movements like a
snake;
And when you think he's half asleep, he's always wide awake.

Macavity, Macavity, there's no one like Macavity,
For he's a fiend in feline shape, a monster of depravity.
You may meet him in a by-street, you may see him in the
square -
But when a crime's discovered, then *Macavity's not there*!

He's outwardly respectable. (They say he cheats at cards.)
And his footprints are not found in any file of Scotland Yard's.
And when the larder's looted, or the jewel-case is rifled,
Or when the milk is missing, or another Peke's been stifled,
Or the greenhouse glass is broken, and the trellis past repair -
Ay, there's the wonder of the thing! *Macavity's not there*!

And when the Foreign Office find a Treaty's gone astray,
Or the Admiralty lose some plans and drawings by the way,
There may be a scrap of paper in the hall or on the stair -
But it's useless to investigate - *Mcavity's not there*!
And when the loss has been disclosed, the Secret Service say:
`It *must* have been Macavity!' - but he's a mile away.
You'll be sure to find him resting, or a-licking of his thumbs,
Or engaged in doing complicated long-division sums.

Macavity, Macavity, there's no one like Macavity,
There never was a Cat of such deceitfulness and suavity.
He always has an alibi, and one or two to spare;
At whatever time the deed took place - MACAVITY WASN'T THERE!
And they say that all the Cats whose wicked deeds are widely known
(I might mention Mungojerrie, I might mention Griddlebone)
Are nothing more than agents for the Cat who all the time
Just controls their operations: the Napoleon of Crime!

TS Eliot 1888 – 1965

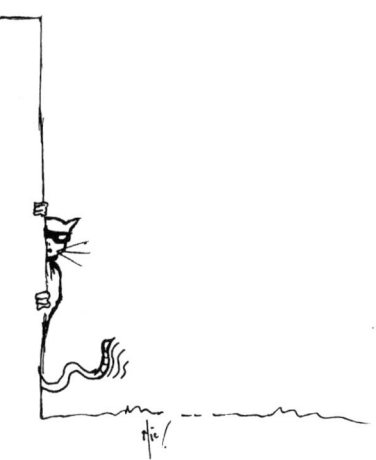

Forwarded by John Middleton's mother, Grace, "she's in her 80's and it makes her laugh" - Shotteswell

Let me live until…..

Today, dear Lord, I'm 80 and
      There's much I haven't done;

I hope, dear Lord, you'll let me live
      Until I'm 81.

But then, if I haven't finished
      All I want to do,

Would you let me stay a while…
      Until I'm 82?

So many places I want to go,
      So very much to see,

Do you think that you could manage
      To make it 83?

The world is changing very fast,
      There's just so much in store,

I'd like it very much to live
      Until I'm 84.

And if by then I'm still alive,
      I'd like to stay till 85…

More plans will be up in the air,
      So I'd really like to stick

And see what happens to the world
      When I am 86.

I know, dear Lord, it's much to ask
        (And it must be nice in heaven)

But I certainly would like to stay
        Until I'm 87.

I know by then I won't be fast,
        And sometimes will be late;

But it truly would be pleasant
        To be around at 88.

I will have seen so many things
        And had a wonderful time.

So, I'm sure that I'll be willing
        To leave at 89 ….maybe!

Mark Cocoran

BILL RICHARDSON

From Cynthia Voisey - Upton
Organist at Ratley and an alto in Ratley's Festival Choir

The Alto's Lament

It's tough to be an alto when you're singing in the choir,
The sopranos get the twiddly bits that people all admire.
The basses boom like loud trombones, the tenors shout with glee,
But the alto part is on two notes, (or if you're lucky, three.)
And when we sing an anthem and lift our hearts in praises
The men get all the juicy bits and telling little phrases.
Of course the trebles sing the tune – they always come off best;
The altos only get three notes and twenty-two bars rest.
We practise very hard each week from hymn book and the Psalter,
But when the conductor looks at us our voices start to falter.
"Too high! Too low! Too fast – you held that note too long!"
It doesn't matter what you do – it's certain to be wrong!
Oh! Shed a tear for altos, they're the Martyrs and they know
In the ranks of choral singers they're considered very low.
They are so very 'umble that a lot of folks forget 'em;
How they'd love to be sopranos, but their vocal chords won't let 'em!
And when the final trumpet sounds and we are wafted higher,
Sopranos, basses, tenors – they'll be in the Heavenly Choir.
While they sing "Alleluia!" to celestial flats and sharps,
The altos will be occupied with polishing the harps.

By "Bob the organist" – enigmatic pen name of a mystery writer

The Car Trip

Mum says:
"Right you two,
This is a very long car journey.
I want you two to be good.
I'm driving and I cant drive properly
if you two are going mad in the back.
do you understand?"

So we say,
"OK Mum, OK. Don't worry"
and off we go.

And we start The Moaning;
Can I have a drink?
I want some crisps.
Can I open my window?
He's got my book.
Get off me.
'Ow thats my ear!

And Mum tries to be exciting:
"Look out of the window
There's a lamp post."

And we go on with The Moaning:
Can I have a sweet?
He's sitting on me.
Are we nearly there?
Don't scratch.
You never tell him off.
Now he's biting his nails.
I want a drink. I want a drink.

And Mum tries to be exciting again:
"Look out of the window
There's a tree."

And we go on:
My hands are sticky.
He's playing with the door handle now.
I feel sick.
Your nose is all runny.
Don't pull my hair.

He's punching me Mum,
That's really dangerous, you know,
Mum he 's spitting.

And Mum says:
"Right ,Im stopping the car.
I AM STOPPING THE CAR."

She stops the car.

"Now if you two don't stop it
I'm going to put you out the car
And leave you by the side of the road."

He started it.
I didn't. He started it.

"I don't care who started it
I can't drive properly
If you two go mad in the back.
Do you understand?"

And we say:
Ok Mum, Ok, don't worry.

Can I have a drink?

Michael Rosen
b. 1946

The Octopus

Tell me, O Octopus, I begs,
Is those things arms, or is they legs?
I marvel at thee, Octopus;
If I were thou, I'd call me Us.

Ogden Nash
1902 - 1971

Somebody

Somebody lives at our house
Though he's never ever seen,
But we often find the traces
Where somebody must have been.

He always breaks our pencils,
And will use our favourite pen.
He takes the tops off tubes of glue,
And doesn't put them back again.

He hides our coats and car keys
And then for work we're late.
He walks the mud into the House,
He never shuts the gate.

He must have lots of socks and gloves
'Cos we've odd ones by the score,
And never can we find a pair
When we search throughout the drawer.

If somebody goes from our House
Things will never be the same,
For at times he is quite useful
When it's really us to blame.

Rene Newey
A friend of the Field family

Warmington W.I.

A gourmet from Warmington Group
Used mixtures of wines in her soup.
When friends came to taste
It was so strongly laced
That they ended by looping the loop.

Helen Smart

છેઠ

From Cynthia and Roger Bayliss – Warmington

Fog

The fog comes
On little cat feet.
It sits looking
Over harbour and city
On silent haunches
And then moves on.

Carl Sandburg
1878 - 1967

Poem Composed in Santa Barbara

The poets talk. They talk a lot.
They talk of T.S. Eliot.
One is anti. One is pro.
How hard they think! How much they know!
They're happy. A cicada sings.
We women talk of other things.

Wendy Cope
b.1945

LAND

The Glory of the Garden

Our England is a garden that is full of stately views,
Of borders, beds and shrubberies and lawns and avenues,
With statues on the terraces and peacocks strutting by;
But the Glory of the Garden lies in more than meets the eye.

For where the old thick laurels grow, along the thin red wall,
You will find the tool- and potting-sheds which are the heart of all;
The cold-frames and the hot-houses, the dungpits and the tanks:
The rollers, carts and drain-pipes, with the barrows and the planks.

And there you'll see the gardeners, the men and 'prentice boys
Told off to do as they are bid and do it without noise;
For, except when seeds are planted and we shout to scare the birds,
The Glory of the Garden it abideth not in words.

And some can pot begonias and some can bud a rose,
And some are hardly fit to trust with anything that grows;
But they can roll and trim the lawns and sift the sand and loam,
For the Glory of the Garden occupieth all who come.

Our England is a garden, and such gardens are not made
By singing:--"Oh, how beautiful!" and sitting in the shade,
While better men than we go out and start their working lives
At grubbing weeds from gravel-paths with broken dinner-knives

There's not a pair of legs so thin, there's not a head so thick,
There's not a hand so weak and white, nor yet a heart so sick.
But it can find some needful job that's crying to be done,
For the Glory of the Garden glorieth every one.

Then seek your job with thankfulness and work till further orders,
If it's only netting strawberries or killing slugs on borders;
And when your back stops aching and your hands begin to harden,
You will find yourself a partner in the Glory of the Garden.

Oh, Adam was a gardener, and God who made him sees
That half a proper gardener's work is done upon his knees,
So when your work is finished, you can wash your hand and pray
For the Glory of the Garden, that it may not pass away!
And the Glory of the Garden it shall never pass away!

Rudyard Kipling
1865 – 1936

The Vagabond

Give to me the life I love,
Let the lave go by me,
Give the jolly heaven above
And the byway nigh me.
Bed in the bush with stars to see,
Bread I dip in the river –
There's the life for a man like me,

There's the life for ever.

Let the blow fall soon or late,
Let what will be o'er me;
Give the face of earth around And the road before me.
Wealth I seek not, hope nor love,
Nor a friend to know me;
All I seek, the heaven above
And the road below me.

Or let autumn fall on me
Where afield I linger,
Silencing the bird on tree,
Biting the blue finger.
White as meal the frosty field –
Warm the fireside haven –
Not to autumn will I yield,
Not to winter even!

Let the blow fall soon or late,
Let what will be o'er me;
Give the face of earth around,
And the road before me.
Wealth I ask not, hope nor love,
Nor a friend to know me;
All I ask, the heaven above
And the road below me.

Robert Louis Stevenson
1850 – 1894

From Daphne Ward - Warmington

The Months of the Year

January brings the snow;
Makes the toes and fingers glow.

February brings the rain,
Thaws the frozen ponds again.

March brings breezes loud and shrill,
Stirs the dancing daffodil.

April brings the primrose sweet,
Scatters daisies at our feet.

May brings flocks with pretty lambs,
Skipping by their fleecy dams.

June brings tulips, lilies, roses;
Fills the children's hands with posies.

Hot July brings cooling showers
Strawberries and gilly-flowers.

August brings the sheaves of corn,
Then the harvest home is borne.

Warm September brings the fruit,
Sportsmen then begin to shoot.

Fresh October brings the pheasant;
Then to gather nuts is pleasant.

Dull November brings the blast,
Then the leaves are falling fast.

Chill December brings the sleet,
Blazing fire and Christmas treat.

Sara Coleridge
1802 – 1852

Woman to Child

You who were darkness warmed my flesh
Where out of darkness rose the seed.
Then all a world I made in me;
All the world you hear and see
Hung upon my dreaming blood.

There hung the multitudinous stars,
And coloured birds and fishes moved.
There swam the sliding continents.
All time lay rolled in me, and sense,
And love that knew not its beloved.

O node and focus of the world;
I hold you deep within that well
You shall escape and not escape-
That mirrors still your sleeping shape;
That nurtures still your crescent cell.

I wither and you break from me;
Yet though you dance in living light
I am the earth, I am the root,
I am the stem that fed the fruit,
The link that joins you to the night.

Judith Wright
1915 – 2000

God Speed the Plough

Let the wealthy and great
Roll in splendour and state
I envy them not I declare it.
I eat my own lamb
My own chickens and ham
I shear my own fleece and I wear it.
I have lawns, I have bowers,
I have fruits, I have flowers,
The lark is my morning alarmer.
So jolly boys now
Here's God speed the plough.
Long life and success to the farmer.

Author unknown

Ducks

From troubles of the world I turn to ducks,
Beautiful comical things
Sleeping or curled
Their heads beneath white wings
By water cool,
Or finding curious things
To eat in various mucks
Beneath the pool,
Tails uppermost, or waddling
Sailor-like on the shores
Of ponds, or paddling
- Left! Right! - with fanlike feet
Which are for steady oars
When they (white galleys) float
Each bird a boat
Rippling at will the sweet
Wide waterway ...
When night is fallen *you* creep
Upstairs, but drakes and dillies
Nest with pale water-stars.
Moonbeams and shadow bars,
And water-lilies:
Fearful too much to sleep
Since they've no locks
To click against the teeth
Of weasel and fox.
And warm beneath
Are eggs of cloudy green
Whence hungry rats and lean
Would stealthily suck
New life, but for the mien
The hold ferocious mien
Of the mother-duck.

R. Tatchell

Yes, ducks are valiant things
On nests of twigs and straws,
And ducks are soothy things
And lovely on the lake
When that the sunlight draws
Thereon their pictures dim
In colours cool.
And when beneath the pool
They dabble, and when they swim
And make their rippling rings,
0 ducks are beautiful things!
But ducks are comical things:-
As comical as you.
Quack!
They waddle round, they do.
They eat all sorts of things,
And then they quack.
By barn and stable and stack
They wander at their will,
But if you go too near
They look at you through black
Small topaz-tinted eyes
And wish you ill.
Triangular and clear
They leave their curious track
In mud at the water's edge,
And there amid the sedge
And slime they gobble and peer
Saying 'Quack! quack!'

When God had finished the stars and whirl of coloured suns
He turned His mind from big things to fashion little ones;
Beautiful tiny things (like daisies) He made, and then
He made the comical ones in case the minds of men
Should stiffen and become
Dull, humourless and glum,
And so forgetful of their Maker be
As to take even themselves - quite seriously.
Caterpillars and cats are lively and excellent puns:
All God's jokes are good - even the practical ones!

And as for the duck, I think God must have smiled a bit
Seeing those bright eyes blink on the day He fashioned it.
And he's probably laughing still at the sound that came out of
its bill!

FW Harvey
1888 – 1953

From Robbie Macfarlane - Ratley

My Old Friend Bill
(Bill Wormell)

My thoughts are aye of you,
We talk about you often over a drink,
You'd approve of that, I think,
My old friend Bill.

You were dry, like Martini,
Sometimes soft, like a comfortable shoe!
We had problems reconciling the two…
Our old friend Bill.

One of the best nights of my life
Was a Tuesday, the 31st of May,
Your 80th birthday – oh what a day!
My older friend Bill.

You still make us smile
We use your expressions, each domino member,
That's a great way to remember
Our dear old friend Bill.

Robbie Macfarlane 1995

Against Idleness and Mischief

How doth the little busy bee
Improve each shining hour,
And gather honey all the day
From every opening flower!

How skilfully she builds her cell!
How neatly spreads the wax!
And labours hard to store it well
With the sweet food she makes.

In works of labour or of skill
I would be busy too;
For Satan finds some mischief still
For idle hands to do.

In books, or work, or healthful play
Let my first years be passed,
That I may give for every day
Some good account at last.

From Divine and Moral Songs
Isaac Watts (1674 – 1748)

Vitai Lampada

There's a breathless hush in the Close tonight -
Ten to make and the match to win –
A bumping pitch and a blinding light,
An hour to play and the last man in.
And it's not for the sake of a ribboned coat,
Or the selfish hope of a season's fame,
But his Captain's hand on his shoulder smote
"Play up! Play up! And play the game!"

The sand of the desert is sodden red –
Red with the wreck of a square that broke –
The Gatling's jammed and the Colonel dead,
And the regiment blind with dust and smoke.
The river of death has brimmed his banks,
And England's far, and Honour a name,
But the voice of a schoolboy rallies the ranks,
"Play up! Play up! And play the game!"

This is the word that year by year
While in her place the School is set
Every one of her sons must hear,
And none that hears it dare forget.
This they all with a joyful mind
Bear through life like a torch in flame,
And falling fling to the host behind –
"Play up! Play up! And play the game!"

Sir Henry Newbolt
1862 - 1938

Selected by Martin Prickett - Shotteswell
John Cole - Warmington   Mark Orr - Ratley

Adlestrop

Yes, I remember Adlestrop --
The name, because one afternoon
Of heat the express-train drew up there
Unwontedly. It was late June.

The steam hissed. Someone cleared his throat.
No one left and no one came
On the bare platform. What I saw
Was Adlestrop -- only the name

And willows, willow-herb, and grass,
And meadowsweet, and haycocks dry,
No whit less still and lonely fair
Than the high cloudlets in the sky.

And for that minute a blackbird sang
Close by, and round him, mistier,
Farther and farther, all the birds
Of Oxfordshire and Gloucestershire.

Edward Thomas 1878-1917
When asked for his choice Martin Prickett wrote:

"I prefer to hear poetry on tape/CD rather than read it and this poem was in either a Classic FM or a BBC compilation of Favourite Poems on audio released about 5 years ago. Having grown up in Shotteswell, I can imagine the calm of a hot summer's day in nearby Adlestrop in Gloucestershire and the luxury of only being able to hear birds, as we could in the valley before the motorway.

"The poem flashed back into my mind on a recent night time journey back home from Bristol when I passed Adlestrop between Stow on the Wold and Chipping Norton. A signpost for the village flashed into my eyes on turning a corner and I immediately felt a sense of privilege to be there and an evocation of hot rural summers."

From Eileen Spencer, Gerald Storer - Shotteswell,
Sally Adams, Jenny Deeming – Warmington
Mark Orr - Ratley

Diary of a Church Mouse

Here among long-discarded cassocks,
Damp stools, and half-split open hassocks,
Here where the Vicar never looks,
I nibble through old service books.
Lean and alone I spend my days
Behind this Church of England baize.
I share my dark forgotten room
With two oil-lamps and half a broom.
The cleaner never bothers me,
So here I eat my frugal tea.
My bread is sawdust mixed with straw;
My jam is polish for the floor.
  Christmas and Easter may be feasts
For congregations and for priests,
And so may Whitsun. All the same,
They do not fill my meagre frame.
For me the only feast at all
Is Autumn's Harvest Festival,
When I can satisfy my want
With ears of corn around the font.
I climb the eagle's brazen head
To burrow through a loaf of bread.
I scramble up the pulpit stair
And gnaw the marrows hanging there.
  It is enjoyable to taste
These items ere they go to waste,
But how annoying when one finds
That other mice with pagan minds
Come into church my food to share
Who have no proper business there.
Two field mice who have no desire
To be baptised, invade the choir.

A large and most unfriendly rat
Comes in to see what we are at.
He says he thinks there is no God
And yet he comes... it's rather odd.
This year he stole a sheaf of wheat
(it screened our special preacher's seat).
And prosperous mice from fields away
Come in to hear the organ play,
And under cover of its notes
Ate through the altar's sheaf of oats.
A Low Church mouse, who thinks that I
Am too papistical, and High,
Yet somehow doesn't think it wrong
To munch through Harvest Evensong,
While I, who starve the whole year through,
Must share my food with rodents who
Except at this time of the year
Not once inside the church appear.
   Within the human world I know
Such goings-on could not be so,
For human beings only do
What their religion tells them to.
They read their Bible every day
And always, night and morning, pray,
And just like me, the good church mouse,
Worship each week in God's own house.
   But all the same it's strange to me
How very full the church can be
With people I don't see at all,
except at Harvest Festival.

**John Betjeman
1906-1984**

Trains

All at once I saw a light
Rumbling noises in the night.
Then I heard the noise of wheels
Catching others on their heels.
Faster, faster goes the train,
Pouring down goes the rain.
Past me there the carriages go
Lights aflickering high and low.
Then all in the still and lonely night
The train went out of sight.

Diana Milroy (Dinny Jones) when age 9

From Jay Williams – Warmington

The Apple

Hanging like a burst of sunrise
An orb, a sphere, a rosy glow,
A joy on which to feast the eyes,
Beyond my grasp from way below,
But then my love reached up for me
And plucked that pippin from the tree.

Jay Williams

Glory of Women

You love us when we're heroes, home on leave,
Or wounded in a mentionable place
You worship decorations; you believe
That chivalry redeems the war's disgrace.
You make us shells. You listen with delight,
By tales of dirt and danger fondly thrilled.
You crown our distant ardours while we fight,
And mourn our laurelled memories when we're killed.
You can't believe that British troops 'retire'
When hell's last horror breaks them, and they run,
Trampling the terrible corpses – blind with blood.
O German mother dreaming by the dire,
While you are knitting socks to send youson
His face is trodden deeper in the mud.

Siegfried Sassoon
1886 - 1967

Snowflake

Falling form the air to join my mates,
Land on the ground,
Safe and sound,
Waiting for kids to appear,
Here they dome wicked,
I get picked up and thrown,
Hit something hard,
And land on the snowy ground,
Children run away,
Where are they going?
The sun comes out and I'm fading away,

NO NOT MEEEEEEEEEEEEEEEEEE!!!!!

David Spencer Age 12

Loveliest of Trees, the Cherry Now

Loveliest of trees, the cherry now
Is hung with bloom along the bough
And stands about the woodland ride
Wearing white for Eastertide
Now, of my threescore years and ten,
Twenty will not come again
And take from seventy springs a score
It only leaves me fifty more
And since to look at things in bloom
Fifty springs are little room
About the woodlands I will go
To see the cherry hung with snow.

A.E. Houseman
1859 – 1936

From Richard Neale, Cynthia and Roger Bayliss –
Warmington.   Deidre Storer – Shotteswell

The Soldier

If I should die, think only this of me:
That there's some corner of a foreign field
That is for ever England. There shall be
In that rich earth a richer dust concealed;
A dust whom England bore, shaped, made aware,
Gave, once, her flowers to love, her ways to roam,
A body of England's, breathing English air,
Washed by the rivers, blest by the suns of home.

And think, this heart, all evil shed away,
A pulse in the eternal mind, no less
Gives somewhere back the thoughts by England given;
Her sights and sounds; dreams happy as her day;
And laughter, learnt of friends; and gentleness,
In hearts at peace, under an English heaven.

Rupert Brooke
1887-1915

From Jean Adams – Warmington

My Best Room

Investing time in the garden
Is always time well spent.
Around me is the beauty
That kindly nature's sent.

With every passing season
The flowers freshly bloom,
Giving me joy and contentment.
The garden's my very best room.

Jean Adams

Fern Hill

Now as I was young and easy under the apple boughs
About the lilting house and happy as the grass was green,
  The night above the dingle starry,
  Time let me hail and climb
  Golden in the heydays of his eyes,
And honoured among wagons I was prince of the apple towns
And once below a time I lordly had the trees and leaves
  Trail with daisies and barley
  Down the rivers of the windfall light.

And as I was green and carefree, famous among the barns
About the happy yard and singing as the farm was home,
  In the sun that is young once only,
  Time let me play and be
  Golden in the mercy of his means,
And green and golden I was huntsman and herdsman, the calves
Sang to my horn, the foxes on the hills barked clear and cold,
  And in the Sabbath rang slowly,
  In the pebbles of the holy streams.

All the sun long it was running, it was lovely, the hay
Fields high as the house, the tunes from the chimneys, it was air,
  And playing, lovely and watery,
  And fire green as grass.
  And nightly under the simple stars
As I rode to sleep the owls were bering the farm away,
All the moon long I heard, blessed among stables, the nightjars
  Flying with the ricks, and the horses,
  Flashing into the dark.

And then to awake, and the farm, like a wanderer white
With the dew, come back, the cock on his shoulder; it was all
   Shining, it was Adam and maiden,
   The sky gathered again
   And the sun grew round that very day.
So it must have been after the birth of the simple light
In the first, spinning place, the spellbound horses walking
warm
   Out of the whinnying green stable
   On to the fields of praise.

And honoured among foxes and pheasants by the gay house
Under the new made clouds and happy as the heart was long,
   In the sun born over and over,
   I ran my heedless ways,
   My wishes raced through the house high hay
And nothing I cared, at my sky blue trades that time allows
In all his tuneful turning so few and such morning songs
   Before the children green and golden
   Follow him out of grace.

Nothing I cared, in the lamb white days, that time would take
me
Up to the swallow thronged loft by the shadow of my hand,
   In the moon that is always rising,
   Nor that riding to sleep
   I should hear him fly with the high fields
And wake to the farm forever fled from the childless land.
Oh, as I was young and easy in the mercy of his means,
   Time held me green and dying
   Though I sang in my chains like the sea.

Dylan Thomas
1914 – 1953

ܐ

Lines Written by a Welsh Stream

I hear water splash against the rocks.
It is soothing. It is quiet.
It is calming. It is peaceful.
I can hear the water trickling,
Dribbling, flowing down,
Rushing, splashing against the edge,
Against mud and silt.

Rosie Houston

This poem was written by a peacekeeping soldier stationed overseas. The following is the author's request –
"PLEASE would you do me the kind honour of sending this to as many people as you can? Christmas will be coming soon and some credit is due to all of the servicemen and women for our being able to celebrate these festivities. Let's try in this small way to pay a tiny bit of what we owe them; make people stop and think of our heroes, living and dead, who sacrifice themselves for us."

Christmas Eve

'Twas the night before Christmas, he lived all alone,
In a one bed-room house made of plaster and stone.
I had come down the chimney with presents to give,
And to see who in this house did live.

I looked all about.   A strange sight I did see:
No tinsel, no presents, not even a tree.
No stocking by the mantle – just boots filled with sand.
On the wall hung pictures of far distant lands.

With medals and badges, awards of all kinds,
A sobering thought came into my mind.
For the house it was different: it was dark and dreary.
I'd found the home of a soldier once I could see clearly.

The soldier lay sleeping, silent, alone,
Curled up on the floor in this one bed-room home.
The face was so gentle, the room in disorder,
Not at all how I pictured the home of a soldier.

Was this the hero of whom I'd just read;
Curled up on a poncho, the floor for a bed?
I realised the families that I saw this night,
Owed their lives to these soldiers who were willing to fight.

Soon round the world the children would play,
And grown-ups would celebrate a bright Christmas Day.
They all enjoyed freedom each month of the year,
Because of the soldiers like the one lying there.

I couldn't help wonder how many lay alone
On a cold Christmas Eve, in a land far from home.
The very thought of it brought a tear in my eye,
I dropped to my knees and started to cry.

The soldier awakened and I heard a gruff voice,
"Santa don't cry.   This life is my choice.
I fight for freedom, I don't ask for more.
My life is my God, my Country, my Corps."

The soldier rolled over and drifted to sleep.
I couldn't control it, I continued to weep.
I kept watch for hours; so silent and still.
And we both shivered from the cold winter's chill.

I didn't want to leave, on that cold dark night,
This guardian of honour so willing to fight.
Then the soldier rolled over, with a voice soft and pure,
Whispered,
"Carry on Santa.   It's now Christmas Day and all is secure"

One look at my watch and I knew he was right.

Merry Christmas my friend and to all – a good night.

From Yve Freer – Radway
Jay Williams - Warmington

The Lake Isle of Innisfree

I will arise and go now, and go to Innisfree,
And a small cabin build there, of clay and wattles made;
Nine bean rows will I have there, a hive for the honey bee,
   And live alone in the bee-loud glade.

And I shall have some peace there, for peace comes dropping slow,
Dropping from the veils of the morning to where the cricket sings;
There midnight's all a glimmer, and noon a purple glow,
   And evening full of the linnet's wings.

I will arise and go now, for always night and day
I hear lake water lapping with low sounds by the shore;
While I stand on the roadway, or on the pavements grey,
   I hear it in the deep heart's core.

W. B. Yeats
1865 - 1939

Wood Fires

Beech wood fires are bright and clear
If the logs are kept a year.
Oaken logs burn steadily
If the wood is old and dry.
Chestnut's only good, they say,
If for long it's laid away.
But ash new or ash old
Is fit for a queen with a crown of gold.

Birch and fir logs burn too fast,
Blaze up bright, but do not last.
Make a fire of elder tree,
Death within your house you'll see.
It is by the Irish said:
Hawthorn bakes the sweetest bread.
But ash green or ash brown
Is fit for a queen with a golden crown.

Elm wood burns like churchyard mould,
E'en the very flames are cold.
Poplar gives a bitter smoke,
Fills your eyes and makes you choke.
Apple wood will scent your room
With an incense like perfume.
But ash wet or ash dry
Is fit or a queen to warm her slippers by.

Anon.

Ratley

A little village on the hill
Where famous battles fought,
In the English country side,
Near to Shakespeare's Court.

This famous Warwick village
Where in upper side I dwell,
Near Compton Wynyates stately Hall,
Called Ratley,on the fell.

It's leafy if the summer time,
And colourful in Spring,
A clean and tidy place to live
Where friends you're pleased to bring.

The Roundheads and the Cavaliers
Passed through here long ago,
Or so the history books do tell,
And we're certain they should know.

It must have been exciting then
To see the soldiers pass,
As on their way to Halford Bridge
Where with steel and ball did clash.

But now we must be up to date
And think in modern tense,
Of industry and rural things
Growing in modest sense.

The Church is still the centre
Of a scene we do espy,
Where not so very far away
The Manse and Inn do lie.

One day I may be leaving,
As yet I know not how,
But I've loved the life in Ratley,
The village of the plough.

R.W. Curwen

The Solitary Reaper

Behold her, single in the field,
  Yon solitary Highland Lass!
Reaping and singing by herself;
  Stop here, or gently pass!
Alone she cuts and binds the grain,
And sings a melancholy strain;
O listen! For the Vale profound
Is overflowing with the sound.

No Nightingale did ever chaunt
  More welcome notes to weary bands
Of travellers in some shady haunt,
  Among Arabian sands:
A voice so thrilling ne'er was heard
In spring-time from the Cuckoo-bird,
Breaking the silence of the seas
Among the farthest Hebrides.

Will no one tell me what she sings? –
  Perhaps the plaintive numbers flow
For old, unhappy, far-off things,
  And battles long ago:
Or is it some more humble lay,
Familiar matter of to-day?
Some natural sorrow, loss, or pain,
That has been, and may be again?

Whate'er the theme, the Maiden sang
  As if her song could have no ending;
I saw her singing at her work,
  And o'er the sickle bending; -
I listen'd, motionless and still;
And, as I mounted up the hill,
The music in my heart I bore,
Long after it was heard no more.

William Wordsworth
1770 – 1850

My Favourite Pet

To write a poem about my pet
Is very difficult for me.
'Cos I have four of them, you see,
And each I love so dearly.
Two of them have four legs,
And two of them have two.
But I really think I must decide
Which one of these will do.

I'll make the youngest one of them,
Holly, my favourite pet.
She's just the sweetest and the cutest
That anyone can get.
She's gentle and quiet, friendly to all,
Her character quite outstanding.
She just delights in playing around
And sometimes is demanding.

She seems to know the time of day
When meal time comes around,
For in her mouth she'll carry her dish,
Wondering perhaps if it's meat or fish.
In her bed she shares with Judy,
Most days you're sure to find
A sock, a slipper or a hat
Or something personal like that.

The things she takes to bed with her
Are not to chew of course,
But just to snuggle up against
And sometimes bury her nose.
I could go on commenting
About Holly, my little pet bitch.
I sincerely hope she'll continue
To amuse without a hitch.

Margaret Martin

Mending Wall

Something there is that doesn't love a wall,
That sends the frozen-ground-swell under it,
And spills the upper boulders in the sun;
And makes gaps even two can pass abreast.
The work of hunters is another thing:
I have come after them and made repair
Where they have left not one stone on stone,
But they would have the rabbit out of hiding,
To please the yelping dogs. The gaps I mean,
No one has seen them made or heard them made,
But at spring mending-time we find them there.
I let my neighbour know beyond the hill;
And on a day we meet to walk the line
And set the wall between us once again.
We keep the wall between us as we go.
To each the boulders that have fallen to each.
And some are loaves and some so nearly balls
We have to use a spell to make them balance:
"Stay where you are until our backs are turned!"
We wear our fingers rough with handling them.
Oh, just another kind of outdoor game,
One on a side. It comes to little more:
He is all pine and I am apple-orchard.
My apple trees will never get across
And eat the cones under his pines, I tell him.
He only says, "Good fences make good neighbours."
Spring is the mischief in me, and I wonder
If I could put a notion in his head:
"Why do they make good neighbours? Isn't it
Where there are cows? But here there are no cows.
Before I built a wall I'd ask to know
What I was walling in or walling out,
And to whom I was like to give offence.

Something there is that doesn't love a wall,
That wants it down!" I could say "Elves" to him,
But it's not elves exactly, and I'd rather
He said it for himself. I see him there,
Bringing a stone grasped firmly by the top
In each hand, like an old-stone savage armed.
He moves in darkness as it seems to me,
Not of woods only and the shade of trees.
He will not go behind his father's saying,
And he likes having thought of it so well
He says again, "Good fences make good neighbours."

Robert Frost
1874-1963

From John Prickett and Gerald Storer – Shotteswell
John Cole   - Warmington

Night Mail

This is the Night Mail crossing the border,
Bringing the cheque and the postal order,
Letters for the rich, letters for the poor,
The shop at the corner and the girl next door.
Pulling up Beattock, a steady climb:
The gradient's against her, but she's on time.
Past cotton-grass and moorland boulder
Shovelling white steam over her shoulder,
Snorting noisily as she passes
Silent miles of wind-bent grasses.
Birds turn their heads as she approaches,
Stare from the bushes at her blank-faced coaches.
Sheep-dogs cannot turn her course;
They slumber on with paws across.
In the farm she passes no one wakes,
But a jug in the bedroom gently shakes.

Dawn freshens, the climb is done.
Down towards Glasgow she descends
Towards the steam tugs yelping down the glade of cranes,
Towards the fields of apparatus, the furnaces
Set on the dark plain like gigantic chessmen.
All Scotland waits for her:
In the dark glens, beside the pale-green sea lochs
Men long for news.

Letters of thanks, letters from banks,
Letters of joy from the girl and the boy,
Receipted bills and invitations
To inspect new stock or visit relations,
And applications for situations
And timid lovers' declarations
And gossip, gossip from all the nations,

News circumstantial, news financial,
Letters with holiday snaps to enlarge in,
Letters with faces scrawled in the margin,
Letters from uncles, cousins, and aunts,
Letters to Scotland from the South of France,
Letters of condolence to Highlands and Lowlands
Notes from overseas to Hebrides
Written on paper of every hue,
The pink, the violet, the white and the blue,
The chatty, the catty, the boring, adoring,
The cold and official and the heart's outpouring,
Clever, stupid, short and long,
The typed and the printed and the spelt all wrong.

Thousands are still asleep
Dreaming of terrifying monsters,
Or of friendly tea beside the band at Cranston's or Crawford's:
Asleep in working Glasgow, asleep in well-set Edinburgh,
Asleep in granite Aberdeen,
They continue their dreams,
And shall wake soon and long for letters,
And none will hear the postman's knock
Without a quickening of the heart,
For who can bear to feel himself forgotten?

W H Auden

1907 – 1973

122

From Sally Adams and Daphne Ward – Warmington
Valerie Scott   - Shotteswell

The Darkling Thrush

I leant upon a coppice gate
When frost was spectre –gray,
And winter's dregs made desolate
The weakening eye of day.
The tangled bine-stems scored the sky
Like strings of broken lyres,
And all mankind that haunted nigh
Had sought their household fires.

The land's sharp features seemed to be
The Century's corpse outleant,
His crypt the cloudy canopy,
And wind his death-lament.
The ancient pulse of germ and birth
Was shrunken hard and dry,
And every spirit upon earth
Seemed fervourless as I.

At once a voice arose among
The bleak twigs overhead
In a full-hearted evensong of joy illimited;
An aged thrush, frail gaunt and small,
In blast-beruffled plume,
Had chosen thus to fling his soul
Upon the growing gloom.

So little cause for carollings
Of such ecstatic sound
Was written on terrestrial things
Afar or nigh around,
That I could think there trembled through
His happy good-night air
Some blessed Hope, whereof he knew
And I was unaware.

Thomas Hardy
1840 – 1928

Ode To Autumn

Seasons of mists and mellow fruitfulness,
Close bosom-friend of the maturing sun;
Conspiring with him how to load and bless
With fruit the vines that round the thatch-eves run;
To bend with apples the moss'd cottage-trees,
And fill all fruit with ripeness to the core;
To swell the gourd, and plump the hazel shells
With a sweet kernel; to set budding more,
And still more, later flowers for the bees,
Until they think warm days will never cease,
For Summer has o'er-brimm'd their clammy cells.

Who hath not seen thee oft amid they store
Sometimes whoever seeks abroad may find
Thee sitting careless on a granary floor,
Thy hair soft-lifted by the winnowing wind;
Or on a half-reap'd furrow sound asleep,
Drows'd with the fume of poppies, while thy hook
Spares the next swath and all its twined flowers:
And sometimes like a gleaner thou dost keep
Steady thy laden head across a brook;
Or by a cyder-press, with patient look,
Thou watchest the last oozings hours by hours.

Where are the songs of Spring? Ay, where are they?
Think not of them, thou hast thy music too, -
While barred clouds bloom the soft-dying day,
And touch the stubble-plains with rosy hue;
Then in a wailful choir the small gnats mourn
Among the river sallows, borne aloft
Or sinking as the light wind lives or dies;
And full-grown lambs loud bleat from hilly bourne;
Hedge-crickets sing; and now with treble soft
The red-breast whistles from a garden-croft;
And gathering swallows twitter in the skies.

John Keats
1795-1821

Pedlars Cottage
(John Middleton's house)

Pedlars cottage
A fairy tale cottage
A great winding drive
The steep sloping roof
Makes it perfect inside
The finishing touches here and there
The flower sweet fragrance fills the air
To add to the fairy tale
A secret garden at the end
A fairy tale cottage
At the quiet village bend

Lottie Hallaways - (niece of John Middleton)
Aged 9 when she wrote this.

I Remember, I Remember

I remember, I remember
The house where I was born,
The little window where the sun
Came peeping in at morn;
He never came a wink too soon
Nor brought too long a day;
But now, I often wish the night
Had borne my breath away.

I remember, I remember
The roses red and white,
The violets and the lily cups –
Those flowers made of light!
The lilacs where the robin built,
And where my brother set
The laburnum on his birthday –
The tree is living yet!

I remember, I remember
Where I was used to swing,
And thought the air must rush as fresh
To swallows on the wing;
My spirit flew in feathers then
That is so heavy now,
The summer pools could hardly cool
The fever on my brow.

I remember, I remember
The fir-trees dark and high;
I used to think their slender tops
Where close against the sky:
It was a childish ignorance,
But now 'tis little joy
To know I'm farther off from Heaven
Than when I was a boy.

Thomas Hood
1799-1845

From Gerald Storer – Shotteswell who wrote: A friend wrote this out for me when I first went abroad in 1952. All the trees had turned brown by 1970.

Young and Old

When all the world is young, lad,
And all the trees are green;
And every goose a swan, lad,
And every lass a queen;
Then hey for boot and horse, lad,
And round the world away;
Young blood must have its course, lad,
And every dog his day.

When all the world is old, lad,
And all the trees are brown;
And all the sport is stale, lad,
And all the wheels run down;
Creep home and take your place there,
The spent and maimed among:
God grant you find one face there,
You loved when all was young.

Charles Kingsley
1819 – 1875

BEECH

Edgehill Fight
(Civil War 1642)

Naked and grey the Cotswolds stand
Beneath the autumn sun,
And the stubble-fields on either hand
Where Stour and Avon run.
There is no change in the patient land
That has bred us every one.

She should have passed in cloud and fire
And save us from this sin
Of war – red war – 'twixt child and sire
Household and kith and kin,
In the heart of a sleepy Midland shire,
With the harvest scarcely in.

But there is no change as we meet at last
On the brow-head or the plain,
And the raw astonished ranks stand fast
To slay or to be slain
By the men they knew in the kindly past
That shall never come again –

By the men they met at dance or chase
In the tavern or the hall,
At the justice-bench and the market-place,
At the cudgel-play or brawl –
Of their own blood and speech and race,
Comrades and neighbours all!

More bitter than death this day must prove
Whichever way it go,
For the brothers of the maids we love
Make ready to lay low
Their sisters' sweethearts, as we move,
Against our dearest foe.

Thank Heaven! At last the trumpet peal
Before our strength gives way.
For King or for the Commonweal –
No matter which they say,
The first dry rattle of new drawn-steel
Changes the world today!.

Rudyard Kipling
1865 – 1936

From Joan Crocker - Shotteswell

Memories

In my childhood days we'd see
Someone bringing us our tea.
We'd listen for his bell, and shout
Hey Mum, the Muffin Man's about.

The milkman would come down the street.
We'd hear the sound of horses' feet.
From churns we'd get our day's supply,
Hurrying lest he passed us by.

Then if on shopping we were sent,
We'd linger with the best intent
To watch the men the butter pat,
Making shapes, some round, some fat.

Then walking further down the street
The smell of coffee would us greet.
There also was a choice of tea,
Which they weighed so carefully.

We've progressed in so many ways
From shopping in those bygone days.
Now everything is packaged tight.
I often wonder if that's right!

Vera May Jefferys
1914 – 1992

Eileen says: "A nice poem to remind us to stop, relax and think."

Leisure

What is life if, full of care,
We have no time to stand and stare.
No time to stand beneath the boughs
And stare as long as sheep or cows.
No time to see, when woods we pass,
Where squirrels hide their nuts in grass.
No time to see, in broad daylight,
Streams full of stars, like skies at night.
No time to turn at Beauty's glance,
And watch her feet, how they can dance.
No time to wait till her mouth can
Enrich that smile her eyes began.
A poor life this if, full of care,
We have no time to stand and stare.

**William Henry Davies
1871 – 1940**

Environmental Friendliness

I want to be a bee.
Their vision is so small they don't see me,
Watching them.
Like God who is so large we don't see him,
Uncomprehending sight.

Furry black and yellow stripy coat,
Tiny wings (how do they hold them up?)
Plunging into scented eastern silks,
Of gorgeous hues.
Rolling, rioting, gorging on the pollen,
Flying home to honey.

Oh how I adore you little bees.
Your vibrant life-enhancing native urge
To pollinate, create and let me know
All's well,
Environmental friendliness exists
In my garden.

Jean Proffitt-White
1941 – 2004

The Voice of Spring

I am coming, I am coming! –
Hark! The little bee is humming!
See, the lark is soaring high
In the blue and sunny sky;
And the gnats are on the wing,
Wheeling round in airy ring.

See the yellow catkins cover
All the slender willows over;
And on banks of mossy green
Star-like primroses are seen;
And, their clustering leaves below,
White and purple violets blow.

Hark! The new-born lambs are bleating,
And the cawing rooks are meeting
In the elm – a noisy crowd;
All the birds are singing loud;
And the first white butterfly
In the sunshine dances by.

Look around thee – look around!
Flowers in all the fields abound;
Every running stream is bright;
All the orchard trees are white;
And each small and waving shoot
Promises sweet flowers and fruit.

Turn thy eyes to earth and heaven
God for thee the spring has given,
Taught the birds their melodies,
Clothed the earth and cleared the skies,
For thy pleasure or thy food –
Pour thy soul in gratitude.

Mary Howitt
1799 - 1888

Cut Grass

Cut grass lies frail:
Brief is the breath
Mown stalks exhale.
Long, long the death.

It dies in the white hours
Of young-leafed June
With chestnut flowers,
With hedges snowlike strewn.

White lilac bowed,
Lost lanes of Queen Anne's lace,
And that high-builded cloud,
Moving at summer's pace.

Philip Larkin
1922-1985

Contributors

Acknowledgements

For kind permission to include copyright material the editors gratefully acknowledge the following:

Bloodaxe Books for *Leaving the Tate* by Fleur Adcock;
Penguin Group for *Headmaster's Hymn* by Allan Ahlberg;
Hodder and Co Ltd for *Diary of a Church Mouse* and *Hoe to Get on in Society* by John Betjeman; (PERMISSION AWAITED)
Dee & Griffin Solicitors for *Leisure* by W.H.Davies;
The Random House Group for *In a Glass of Cider, Mending Wall* and untitled *Forgive my little jokes on thee* from the POETRY OF ROBERT FROST edited by Edward Connery Latham, published by Jonathan Cape;
Sheil Land Associates Ltd for *Time* and *If I Should Go* by Joyce Grenfell;
The Society of Authors for *Loveliest of Trees* by A.E. Houseman;
Curtis Brown Ltd. for *To Someone Who Insisted I Look Up Someone* by X.J.Kennedy;
Cherry Large for *To a Grandmother* by Sophie Large;
The Society of Authors for *Cargoes* by John Masefield;
Spike Milligan Publications for *On the Ning Nang Nong* by Spike Milligan;
Peters, Fraser and Dunlop for *Celia Celia* by Adrian Mitchell;
John Murray Publishers for *The Highwayman* by Alfred Noyes;
David Higham Associates for *For Johnny* by John Pudney
George Sassoon for *Glory of Women* by Siegfried Sassoon ("*Copyright Siegfried Sassoon by kind permission of George Sassoon*");
J.M. Dent an imprint of The Orion Publishing Group for *The Kingdom* by R.S. Thomas.
A.P.Watt for *An Irish Airman Foresees his Death* and *The Lake isle of Innisfree* by W.B.Yeats;

Every effort has been made to obtain the necessary permissions but the editors apologise for any errors or omissions in the above list.